A Guide to Soccer and Coaching

Ade's Way

Adrian Webster

Copyright © 2018 Adrian Webster

All rights reserved.

ISBN-13:978-1725674110

ISBN-10:1725674114

Excerpt from A Guide to Soccer and Coaching

The first thing I thought about with a view to doing the coaching book, was that I wanted it to be different. So I have attempted to put together a book that shares my views and experiences of having been involved in the game as a player, coach and manager at youth, college and pro levels.

I started to get involved in coaching when I first joined the Seattle Sounders in 1974. I remember my coach, John Best, saying to me at the time, that soccer was still a relatively new sport in America. He felt that because we grew up playing the game in England and because football/soccer was the biggest sport over there, we already had an advantage over the players and coaches that we would be working with. Because you have played the game, doesn't necessarily make you a good coach, so another thing I took on-board from Coach Best, was to become more aware of how we learn and that coaching is very much like teaching. So, good verbal communication and visual demonstrations became my focus and as they say, *a picture paints a thousand words.*

A GUIDE TO SOCCER AND COACHING: ADE'S WAY

Table of Contents

A Guide to Soccer and Coaching i
Ade's Way i
Excerpt from A Guide to Soccer and Coaching iii
CONTENTS .... **Error! Bookmark not defined.**
DEDICATION 7
ADRIAN WEBSTER CAREER 9
INTRODUCTION 11
MY TEAM 15
HOW I WANT MY TEAM TO PLAY 18
CONTROL, PASS AND MOVE 20
UNDERSTANDING OF INDIVIDUAL ROLES . 24
A FEW SOCCER TIPS 36
TEAM SHAPE 38
ADE'S WAY 44
PRINCIPLES OF SOCCER 46
DEFENDING 48
MIDFIELD PLAY 49
ATTACKING PLAY 50
SYSTEMS OF PLAY 52
PATTERNS OF PLAY 59
COACHING YOUTH SOCCER 69
COACHING W/O PLAYING EXPERIENCE 71
TECHNIQUE 74
HOW TO SETUP 80
TACTICS 81
PHYSICAL FITNESS 83
PSYCHOLOGY–MENTAL ALERTNESS 88
PRE-SEASON 90
SUMMARY 92
MY TEN SOCCER COMMANDMENTS 94
DEFENDING AND ATTACKING PRINCIPLES 96
SPECIAL THANKS 97
ABOUT THE AUTHOR 98
Books to Go Now 102

ADRIAN WEBSTER

DEDICATION

I would like to dedicate this book to several people who had an impact on my football/soccer career. The first is my dad, who was always supportive and encouraged me to follow my dream. I think the first real coaching I got was from my PE (Physical Education) teacher, Peter Hurst, who went above and beyond for me and my schoolmates. My introduction to the pro game was through John Chandler who was my Manager/Coach when playing for Colchester United Youth Team. While I was at Colchester United, there were two senior pros that would later help me make the decision to go to Vancouver in May 1972: Roy Massey my Tiptree Manager and Bobby Cram who was player coach for the Vancouver Spartans. While I played for the Spartans, two people came into my life when I got an offer to go and play for the Seattle Sounders in the NASL. They were John Best and Jimmy Gabriel. They were without doubt the two biggest influences on my playing career and why I got involved in coaching and management.

When I returned to England, I caught up with an old teammate, Steve Foley, who introduced me to John Schultz and between them, they got me back involved at Colchester United where I worked in the youth setup for thirteen years.

Unfortunately, some are no longer with us, but I would like to say a big thank you for all the help and support they gave me along the way.

Great Memories!

Ade

ADRIAN WEBSTER CAREER

Playing career

1968 – 1982   Colchester United England

Hillingdon Borough England

Vancouver Spartans Canada

Seattle Sounders USA

Pittsburgh Spirit USA

Phoenix Inferno USA

Coaching career

1982 – 1987   Phoenix Inferno

Phoenix Sports Centre

Scottsdale Community College

1988 – 1990   Arizona Condors

General Manager/Head Coach

1991 – 1992   Brightlingsea Utd FC.   Manager

1992 – 1993	Halstead Town FC.	Manager
1993 – 2006	Colchester United FC.	
	Summer Camp Coordinator	
	Soccer Centre Manager	
	Centre of Excellence U16 Manager	
	Recruitment Officer	
	YDO / C of E Manager U9 - 16	
2006 – 2016	Colne Community College Assistant Director of Football.	

INTRODUCTION

I recently visited Seattle to celebrate the 40th Anniversary of Soccer Bowl '77 and to promote the books I had published about my time with the Sounders. During the visit, I met with my dear friend, Jenni Conner, who had published my books, and we talked about doing more.

The first fruit of these discussions was *Circle of Life,* which compiled and updated some of the highlights from my first two books, as well as a piece about my visit to Seattle. It is available to buy on Amazon. Jenni and I also talked about doing a coaching book, and whilst my initial reaction was that I thought there were already many books and other coaching resources out there, I promised to give it some thought when I got back to England.

The first thing I thought about with a view to doing the coaching book, was that I wanted it to be different. So I have attempted to put together a book that shares my views and experiences of having been involved in the game as a player, coach and manager at youth, college and pro levels.

I started to get involved in coaching when I first joined the Seattle Sounders in 1974. I remember my coach, John Best, saying to me at the time, that soccer was still a relatively new sport in America. He felt that because we grew up playing the game in England and because football/soccer was the biggest sport over there, we already had an advantage over the players and coaches that we would be working with. Because you have played the game, doesn't necessarily make you a good coach, so another thing I took on-board from Coach Best, was to become more aware of how we learn and that coaching is very much like teaching. So, good verbal communication and visual demonstrations became my focus and as they say, *a picture paints a thousand words*.

I was very lucky during my six seasons playing for the Sounders as I had some great role models in coaches Best, Gabriel, Howe and Redknapp. Many of the ideas I have formed about the game, I got from studying the strengths and weaknesses of these coaches as well as other coaches and managers that I have worked with over the years.

When coaching professional players, obviously it is important to have a good understanding of the game, but I think the one ingredient coaches Best, Gabriel, Howe and Redknapp all had, was being able to get the best out of their players and their man management skills were very good!

Throughout my career, there have been many highs and lows, so when I am coaching, I feel I can relate much better to the player and the team. This is because I know how it feels to be rejected, to sit on the bench, to be injured, to play in a championship game, in front of big crowds of 50,000 to 70,000 and the not-so-big crowds, as well as to play with and against some of the best players in the world, and how it feels to win or lose a game.

When gathering my thoughts on how I could make this book different, I thought I would take a look at coaching kids seven to twelve years old, youth players thirteen to nineteen years old and senior players and pros. Again, this is based on my soccer journey and what I have experienced throughout my career that spans over fifty years!

Adrian Webster and Pele in Soccer Bowl '77

MY TEAM

Soccer is a team sport and ideally, my team would consist of players that are coachable, able to take on-board the information they are given and apply it in both training and games. Training is about developing good habits and prepares you for your match play.

The type of player I am looking for should be enthusiastic and have a positive attitude to both training and playing.

As the coach, it is my responsibility to create a healthy and learning working environment, whereby players are encouraged to express themselves without fear of making mistakes.

Being comfortable with the ball is very important to how I want my team to play and at sixteen years old, I feel that players should be technically sound.

Soccer is not rocket science and for players to improve their game, they need to work with the ball. Being able to use both feet will afford you a bit more time and space. The game is made up of defending and attacking principles and I want my players to be able to make the transition when losing or regaining possession of the ball. Therefore, players need to have a good understanding of the principles required in both defending and attacking.

Players are required to perform to the best of their ability for a period of up to ninety minutes, therefore it is very important that the team has a good fitness base. I want my team to play at a high tempo, but also to be able to slow it down and keep possession when needed. Players need to know how their body works and the importance of a healthy diet, as well as rest to help their recovery so they are able to do it all over again. For me, fitness is the foundation to putting together an entertaining and winning team.

When coaching kids, the coach should not lose sight that it is a development program. For players sixteen to nineteen years, we are preparing them to make the step up to senior football and I believe they have to earn the right to start. I don't think there is anything wrong in developing a winning mentality.

For every winning team, there has to be a losing team, therefore my emphasis will be on trying to get the performance right because I believe that if you do so more often than not, the result will go hand in glove. Sometimes, you will be the better team and still not get the result, which I can accept if I feel we have given it our best effort and tried to do it the right way.

Once we have established a good fitness base, I will put forward to the team how I would like them to play, making sure they understand clearly our strategy. It is important that I keep an open mind and allow the players to have an input, as I want them to believe and sign up to what our goals are for the season.

At the time of starting to write this book, I was still working with college players sixteen to nineteen years old. Most of the players coming into the program are technically quite good. Their fitness levels vary, but where I think their game breaks down, is in a lack of understanding of their individual roles.

When putting your team together, I think before establishing what system or how you want to play, you have to take a look at the strengths and weaknesses of the players you are working with. I also like to balance the team out with a few natural left-sided players.

HOW I WANT MY TEAM TO PLAY

I want my team to be a forward-thinking team that asks questions of the opposition.

Control, pass and move will be the foundation of our team strategy. However, players will also be encouraged to express their individual skills in the right areas.

As I have already mentioned, the game is not rocket science and is made up of defending and attacking principles. Defending starts as soon as you lose possession and attacking, as soon as you regain possession. Players must understand they have a part to play in both defending and attacking.

In the game you are under pressure in 3 ways: your opponent, time and space. The best players are the ones that make the right decisions more often.

Goals and clean sheets win games. Good possession gives you a better chance. Good preparation is therefore the key to giving your team the best possible chance.

I would like for my team to try to play out from the back when it is on to do so. Trusting your teammates and an understanding of your role, is important in good buildup play. An early picture and a good first touch will help your decision-making.

At some point in the game, regardless of your position, you will be under pressure and I think every player should have in their repertoire a move or two to get themselves out of trouble. When receiving the ball, try not to panic, think *'control and manoeuvre.'* Doing so, will afford you a bit more time and space. If your first touch is forward, be positive and look to pass or run the ball forward. Remember, the ball will never get tired and it can travel quicker than you, so make the ball do the work.

Within our team structure, I like to work on patterns of play, so players can get a better understanding of good support. The angle, distance, and the timing of the run, are all key to good support.

When being marked, make your first movement away from the ball and when checking back to receive it, try to be sideways on. This way, you can see where the ball is coming from and where you want to go with it.

CONTROL, PASS AND MOVE

Control. There are two ways of bringing the ball under control. They are *Cushion control* and *Wedge control*. When bringing the ball under control think Control and Manoeuvre. This affords you a bit more time and space. Cushion control is taking the pace off of the ball using your foot, thigh, chest or head by relaxing on contact with the ball. With Wedge control it is about getting your body behind the ball and placing the body surface over the ball to stop it bouncing back up at you. When having the ball under control you have two options: you can either run with it or pass it.

Pass. A good first touch and an early picture aids your decision-making. You don't have to be a George Best and be able to dribble the ball around half a dozen players. You can accomplish that with one well executed pass of the ball. When making a pass, coaches will talk about pass consideration—accuracy and pace of the pass. If you are not accurate, but the pace or the weight of the pass is right, the player looking to receive it can always get to it. An early picture will help determine whether you play the ball into his feet or into the space. Distance will determine the type of pass and you have three basic choices:

1. *Push pass* using the inside of the foot over a short distance.

2. *Driven pass* using the lace area of the boot – played more firmly to prevent interception.

3. With the *Lofted* or *Chip pass,* you use the big toe area of your foot looking to play the ball to a teammate through the air. With the Chip pass, there is no follow through. This gets the ball up quickly over the midfield area and because it is clipped, it puts back spin on the ball and it fades into the path of the receiver.

When making a pass, make your first look forward and when trying to penetrate the opposition's defence, play it with a bit more pace so not to get intercepted. Good control and passing equals good possession!

Move. Movement asks questions of the opposition. We encourage players to move after making a pass to do two things:

1. To give his teammate the option of playing the ball back to him, or;

2. To play the ball into the space he has created for another teammate to come into that space. It doesn't have to be a thirty-yard run but by just changing the angle it gives your teammate another option.

Good passing and movement (combination play) in and around the penalty area makes it difficult to defend against. When receiving the ball and laying it off, make your first movement away from the ball. This asks questions of the defender who now has to make a decision whether to stay with you or to defend the space. When looking to exploit the space, a change of pace makes it even more difficult for the defender.

A GUIDE TO SOCCER AND COACHING: ADE'S WAY

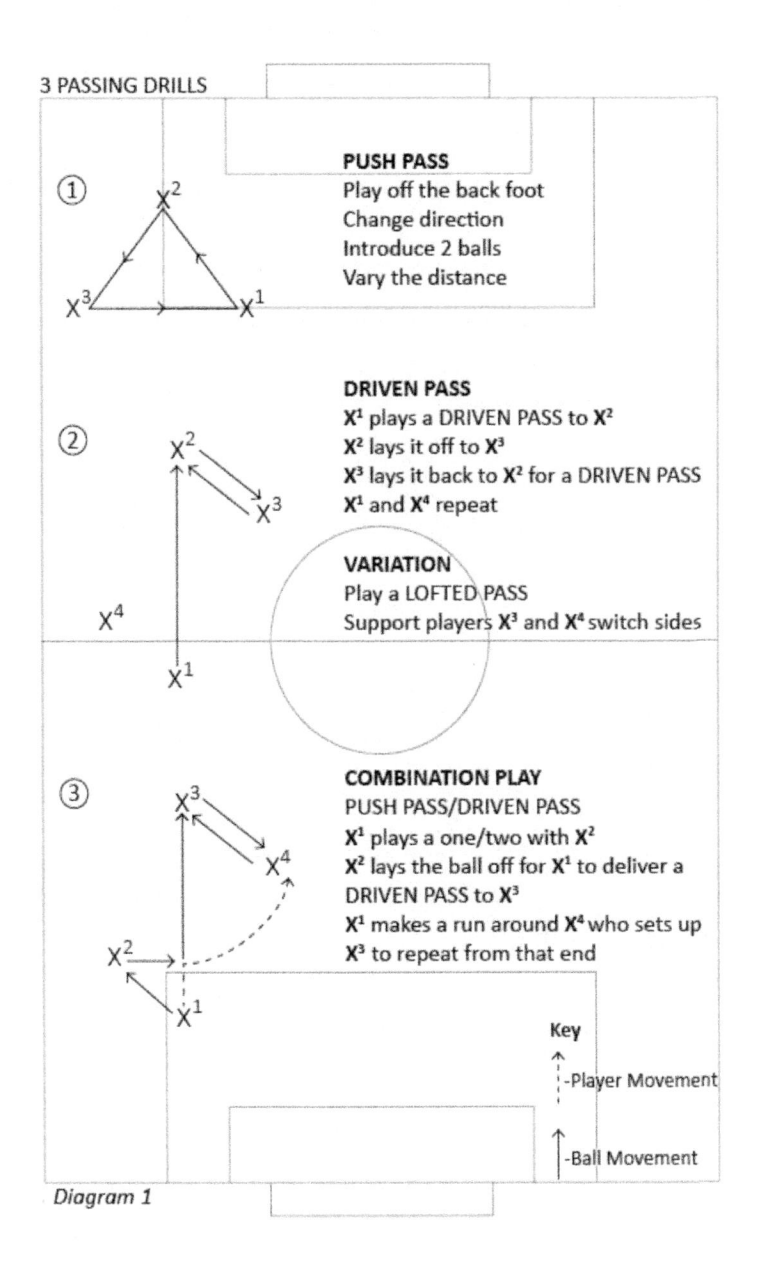

3 PASSING DRILLS

①

PUSH PASS
Play off the back foot
Change direction
Introduce 2 balls
Vary the distance

②

DRIVEN PASS
X^1 plays a DRIVEN PASS to X^2
X^2 lays it off to X^3
X^3 lays it back to X^2 for a DRIVEN PASS
X^1 and X^4 repeat

VARIATION
Play a LOFTED PASS
Support players X^3 and X^4 switch sides

③

COMBINATION PLAY
PUSH PASS/DRIVEN PASS
X^1 plays a one/two with X^2
X^2 lays the ball off for X^1 to deliver a DRIVEN PASS to X^3
X^1 makes a run around X^4 who sets up X^3 to repeat from that end

Key
-Player Movement
-Ball Movement

Diagram 1

UNDERSTANDING OF INDIVIDUAL ROLES

Something that I can't repeat enough is that it is important for players to understand the job that they have to do within the team, and that begins with thinking about their positions. There are several formations available to soccer strategists, but at the basic level, this includes the following broad positions: a goalkeeper, defenders, midfielders, and forwards (forwards are sometimes also referred to as 'strikers' or 'attackers').

Whilst those familiar with soccer should already be aware of this, for anyone new to the game - such as a coach transitioning to soccer from another sport, or for a novice player just beginning to learn - this knowledge might not be so obvious. For the sake of clarity, this is how the positions mentioned above can typically align in a traditional '4-4-2' formation, although there are many variations to this line-up depending on tactical choices, which I will explain later in this book:

```
                         GOALKEEPR

RIGHT BACK    CENTRE BACK    CENTRE BACK    LEFT BACK

RIGHT WING    CENTRE MID.    CENTRE MID.    LEFT WING

                    FORWARD   FORWARD
```

Now let's look at each position in a bit more depth:

GK (Goalkeeper). The primary job of the GK is to stop the ball from going into the back of the net. However, I want my GK to play a more important role and to be the Keeper/Sweeper. Therefore, I would expect him to be equally comfortable with the ball at his feet.

Most keepers I have played with have been good shot stoppers and their main weakness has been dealing with crosses. I want my keeper to have good agility and to be brave. When dealing with crosses, read the flight of the ball, leave it late and come quickly. Good lateral movement is important, do not cross your feet over.

When in possession of the ball, get to the edge of the box quickly, looking to setup a quick counterattack. Good communication is also important. Don't allow your defenders to drop too deep. As well as being the last line of defence, he can also be the first line of offence, so a good starting position is essential. A good first touch and being able to use both feet, is also a bonus!

DEFENDERS FB (Full Back – a term used to describe the right back and left back positions either side of the central defenders). I want my FB's to be able to play from box to box. Therefore, they need to have a good understanding of defending and attacking principles, as well as have good speed endurance. When I first started to play FB, I was encouraged to take up a wide position when the keeper had the ball and told to get the ball into the front players and to push up quickly.

When I went to play for the Seattle Sounders, both coaches, Best and Gabriel, talked about and showed me the importance of the quality of the service into the front players. I had the habit of trying to hit the inch perfect pass and it was Jimmy Gabriel who told me to just try to drop the ball into the space in front of the receiver to come onto it. He showed me how to get the ball up quickly over the midfield and how to put backspin on the ball so it would fade into the space in front of my target.

In my first couple of seasons of playing FB, I was told to support the wide player in front of me from behind so that if he was unable to get his cross in, I was available for him to roll the ball back for me to play it into the penalty area from a slightly deeper position. Another thing we worked on was the timing of the overlap and the delivery of the the ball in the attacking third where the emphasis was to miss out the first defender with the cross. In today's modern game FBs or Wing Backs, are more evident than the good old-fashioned wingers who made a living taken on the FB and getting his cross in. I also remember early on, many of my crosses ending up behind the goal and again it was Coach Gabriel telling me to make my last touch before crossing it slightly inside as well as showing me how to deliver the ball Beckham-like (not quite as effective as Beckham), by hitting across the ball which bends the ball away from the keeper and defenders into the path of the attacking players.

As a FB, you are often up against quick players, so good pace is important. Not only are you expected to get forward when the ball is on your side of the field, you are also responsible for providing cover for your CBs when the opposition are attacking on the other side of the field. Your body shape and movement of your head enables you to see both the ball and your opponent. A lot of crosses delivered into the penalty area are hit deep, so the FB needs to be a good header of the ball.

CB (Centre-back – *a term used to describe the defenders positioned centrally or inside the full-backs.*

***Sometimes also referred to as Central Defenders*).** The qualities that I look for in a good CB are pace/mobility, a good range of passing and good in the air. Playing CB quite often means you are matched up against the opposition's key player who is either mobile and scores goals or is a big strong target man and usually an aerial threat. The key to good defending is to stop your opponent from turning. Don't dive in, stay on your feet. By marking goal side and ball side, you stand less chance of getting boxed in and you might be able to step in front of your opponent to intercept the ball. Good use of the ball is very important in playing out from the back and a good range of passing is key to trying to exploit the opposition's defensive setup.

Height can also be an asset and having good spring when competing for the ball in the air, is something all CBs need to work on in training.

MIDFIELD (Wing play). In the 4-4-2 diagram, wing play would normally be the responsibility of the right- and left-sided midfielders, but in other formations, it might be the job of the FBs, which I will explain later. The primary job of the winger is to provide crosses into the penalty box. Playing out wide can be very frustrating at times as there can be long periods when you are not involved and all you seem to be doing is tracking back. You have to remember the game is made up of defending and attacking principles and all players are required to work hard in and out of possession of the ball. Pace is a big asset and being able to run at pace with the ball at a defender is a defender's worst nightmare. When playing a 4-4-2, I think it is very important to try to develop good partnerships. Perhaps the best example of a FB and Winger partnership I can share, is that of the two ex-Manchester Utd. players, Gary Neville and David Beckham. If you watched Beckham play in a wide position you would very seldom see him go by his opponent. But what he was very good at, was creating that half a yard of space and delivering the perfect cross or dragging the ball away from the FB, knocking it into the front man and going and getting it back off of him. I loved to watch Manchester Utd. play when they had Beckham on one wing and Giggs on the other side. Two completely different styles! Giggs had the ability to run and dribble with the ball at pace, he could go outside and get his cross in or go inside and get his shot off. What I liked about both was that they were each prepared to do the dirty side of the game in tracking back to help out on defence.

When defending in our own defensive third and our keeper regains possession of the ball, I want my two wide players to hit the half way line as quickly as possible. This does two things:

1. We may be able to hit the opposition on the counter attack if their players are lazy in tracking back, or;

2. By doing so, we also create space for our FBs to come

into and we can look to play out from the back.

When making the run to receive the ball get your head up to observe what your options are should you receive it. A good first touch out from under your feet will help you to travel quickly with the ball. Continue to look up after each touch. This will help your decision-making. I think having a few moves and a change of pace in your locker makes it more difficult for your opponent.

When the ball is being manoeuvred down one wing I am looking for the winger on the opposite side to time his run and to get in around the back. This also asks questions of the FB on that side who is also trying to provide cover as well as keep an eye on his opponents movement. As the player on the ball gets his head down to deliver the ball, the opposite winger should look to pull away again to give himself time to adjust to the flight and the pace of the cross coming in. By doing this, wingers are able to get shots and headers on target and if the angle is right, maybe get on the score sheet.

CM (Central Midfielders). When I played in midfield it was as a holding midfielder and my job was to screen the back four, win my tackles and to give it to the more creative players. It was a bonus that I was able to use both feet and had a good range of passing as well as being decent in the air. As a three in midfield, we had a nice balance of an attacking midfielder, a holding midfielder and a creative midfielder (Jenkins/Hudson,

Webster and Buttle). We would use the centre circle as a guide to help keep our shape and balance as well as create good angles and distance of support. As the holding midfielder (and because I played behind the other two) communication was very important, and as a unit we tried to keep the play in front of us. The two attacking midfield players that I played with during my time with the Sounders were Tommy Jenkins and Alan Hudson. Both were very good at running at the opposition and committing them by playing into and off of our front players. Huddy was particularly good at disguising his pass and then going to get the ball back again. Steve Buttle used to say to me, "You win it and give it to me." He was very good at finding pockets of space. He was also very comfortable with the ball, and very seldom gave it away. His decision-making was very good, and he was excellent at making those penetrating passes. Unfortunately the unit of Hudson, Webster and Buttle did not play a great number of games together due to injuries and the players' strike (see my previous book, *Circle of Life*). However, when I got into coaching I started to think how I could develop a rotation of my three central midfielders to ask questions of the opposition and to balance the work load when defending as a unit.

Midfield is the link between the defenders and forwards and angles and distance of support is very important. When receiving the ball, try to get sideways on and receive it on your back foot. A good first touch and an early picture helps your decision-making and whenever possible try to run or pass the ball forward. I once worked with a coach who used to drill it into his players to pass the ball square and back to keep possession so much it made the opposition's job of defending easy. I used to say to him if that's the way you want your team to play then you should move the goals to the side of the pitch. My point being it is those penetrating passes and forward runs with the ball that asks questions of the opposition. Be brave and in the final third, don't be frightened to take chances.

In putting my midfield unit together, I would also be looking for that player who is going to kick in with ten to fifteen goals a season (a Stephen Gerrard or a Frank Lampard). The midfield is often referred to as the 'engine room' and players like Gerrard and Lampard would cover a lot of ground, therefore a good fitness base is essential. I think the key to having a rounded midfield is discipline and an understanding of your role.

FWDS (Forwards). I personally don't like to play with just one up top, but much prefer a partnership or a unit of three. No matter how we setup, I want my front players to be mobile because movement causes problems for defenders. Obviously, certain players bring different qualities to the table and it is all about how the coach utilises each player's strengths. Whether we play with two or three up front I want one of those players to be a good target man, someone we can play the ball into and off of as well as hold it up for us in tight situations and to also be an aerial threat.

In reaching the Soccer Bowl Final in 1977, our front two were Tommy Ord and Micky Cave. Although Tommy was not particularly tall for a forward, he had good spring, he would jump early and he had the knack of being able to hang. He was also a good target man for us, someone you could play into and off of, he also had a good first touch, could hold it up under pressure and he scored goals. Micky Cave was a different type of player who was good at playing between defenders and off the shoulder of his opponent, enabling him to make those darting little runs in behind the defence. I thought they were a very good partnership and one of the main reasons we got to the Final. Although their primary job was to score goals, which was how they got the accolades, they also had defensive responsibilities. When the opposition's GK had the ball, they would drop off together, thereby encouraging the opposition to play out from the back. When the ball was rolled out to one of the defenders, the nearest one would look to apply pressure by looping his run and to show him inside, the other player would then drop off to stop the forward pass. This did two things for us:

1. It kept the play in front of us.

2. It afforded our midfield and defenders to take up good defending shape and balance.

This is very much how I want my front players to apply their defending responsibilities back to the halfway line. I'm not particularly bothered about them chasing all the way back into our own penalty box, because we should still have seven to eight outfield players plus the GK and if we are organised, we should be okay. Remember, if we leave two players up, they will probably leave three back plus the GK, so we still have a numerical advantage of 9 V 7. By doing this, we can perhaps give the front players a little bit more recovery time allowing them to be more dynamic in and around the opposition's penalty box.

In the attacking third, I want my players to take chances and the one thing I always say to them is, 'The goal never moves.' I try to encourage them to get sideways on when receiving the ball so they can protect it better, see where it's coming from and where they want to go with it. When getting shots and headers off, it is important to work the keeper and to follow up for rebounds! Another thing I am not really keen on is my front players making runs into the wide channels. I tell them to leave the channels open for the wide players you just look to get into the box. If I am playing with two wide players, I want the non-crossing winger to also look at getting into the box. That way, we are able to attack the near, middle and far post areas.

A FEW SOCCER TIPS

1. Defensively, instead of getting too tight on your opponent mark him at arm's length and just as he is about to receive the ball, reach out and tap him. This will just break his concentration and he may miss control the ball.
2. As a forward and the ball is being played into you just before you come off towards it, step back into the defender (perhaps stepping on his foot), but don't make it look obvious. This will give you an advantage when looking to control the ball or to flick it on if it is in the air.
3. When dribbling or running with the ball at a defender, encourage the player to attack the defender's front foot. The best he can do is to try to flick it away.
4. If you do not have a training partner to practice with find a wall. You can work on your touch, passing, heading, control and accuracy.
5. Lofted pass: two players stand twenty yards either side of a full-size goal, eight feet high by eight yards wide and practice dropping the ball into the space in front of each other. Vary the distance.

6. When coaching young players, one of the hardest things to get them to do is to communicate. Try taking all communication away from them, no talking, calling for the ball, whistling or waving arms. After doing this for a while, give it back to them. I think you will be surprised at how many of them are now trying to communicate one way or another.

TEAM SHAPE

The mechanics of team shape is like breathing in and out.

Breathing in and (expanding) to provide width and create our attacking shape.

Breathing out and (contracting) to get our defensive shape—compactness and balance.

Good team shape requires:

1. Good support—linking the defence, midfield and forwards.
2. Angles and distance between players.
3. An understanding of how offside is dealt with collectively.
4. Utilisation of width—in attacking mode or compactness defensively.

From a strategy perspective in keeping good team shape and balance, think in terms of thirds of the pitch.

Attacking third: Positive attitude, take risks.

Middle third: Build-up zone, keeping possession. Decision-making when to play forward.

Defending third: The no-nonsense zone. Safety first.

Possession of the ball is very important, but it does not necessarily win you games. Goals and clean sheets win games!

When I first came back from America, I went to watch my nephew play. He played CM and on the ball, he looked a very good player. However, like many young players, he didn't really have a good understanding of his role and he wanted to be everywhere the ball was. Consequently, when he got into the final third where he needed that bit of quality, he was too tired to have an impact. After the game I spoke with the coach and we agreed that the 4–4–2 he wanted them to play looked a bit disjointed. He asked me if I would do a session on the board with them and then take it out onto the pitch.

Diagram 2 — 4-4-2

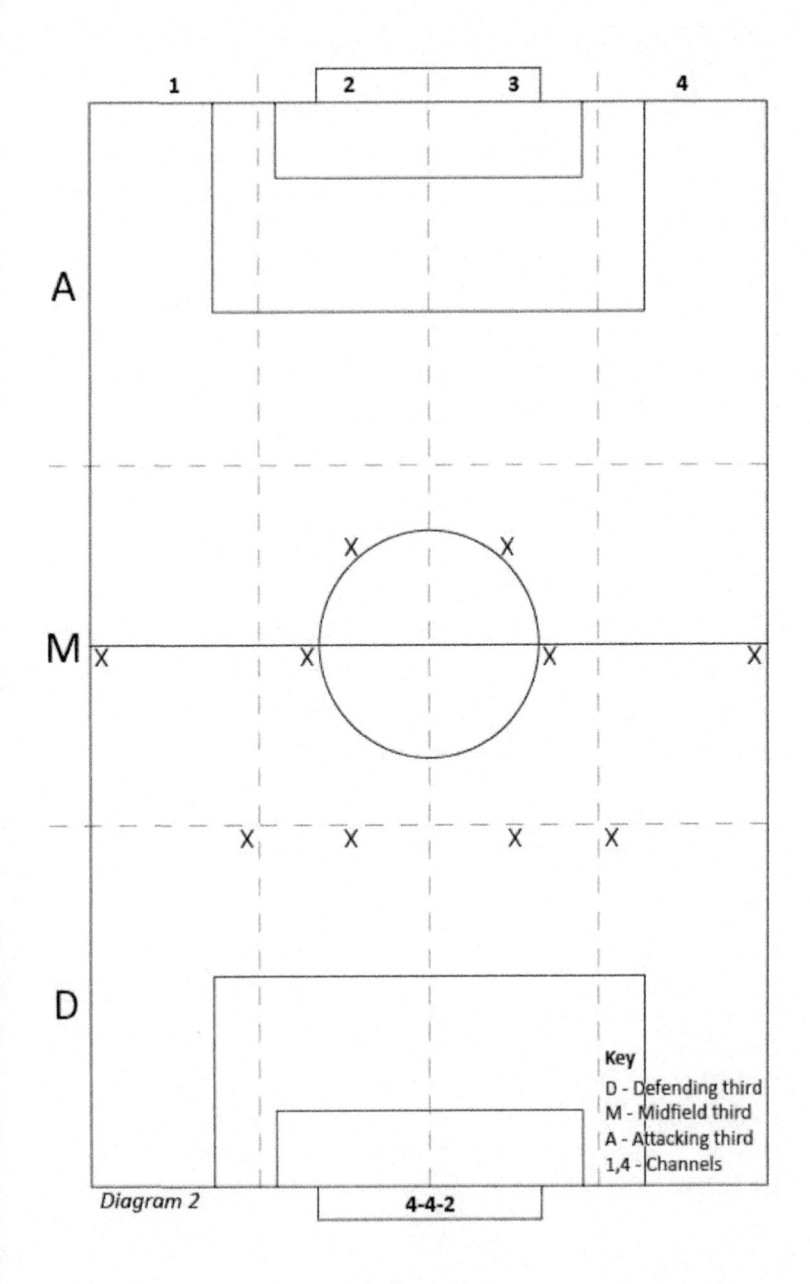

Key
D - Defending third
M - Midfield third
A - Attacking third
1,4 - Channels

A GUIDE TO SOCCER AND COACHING: ADE'S WAY

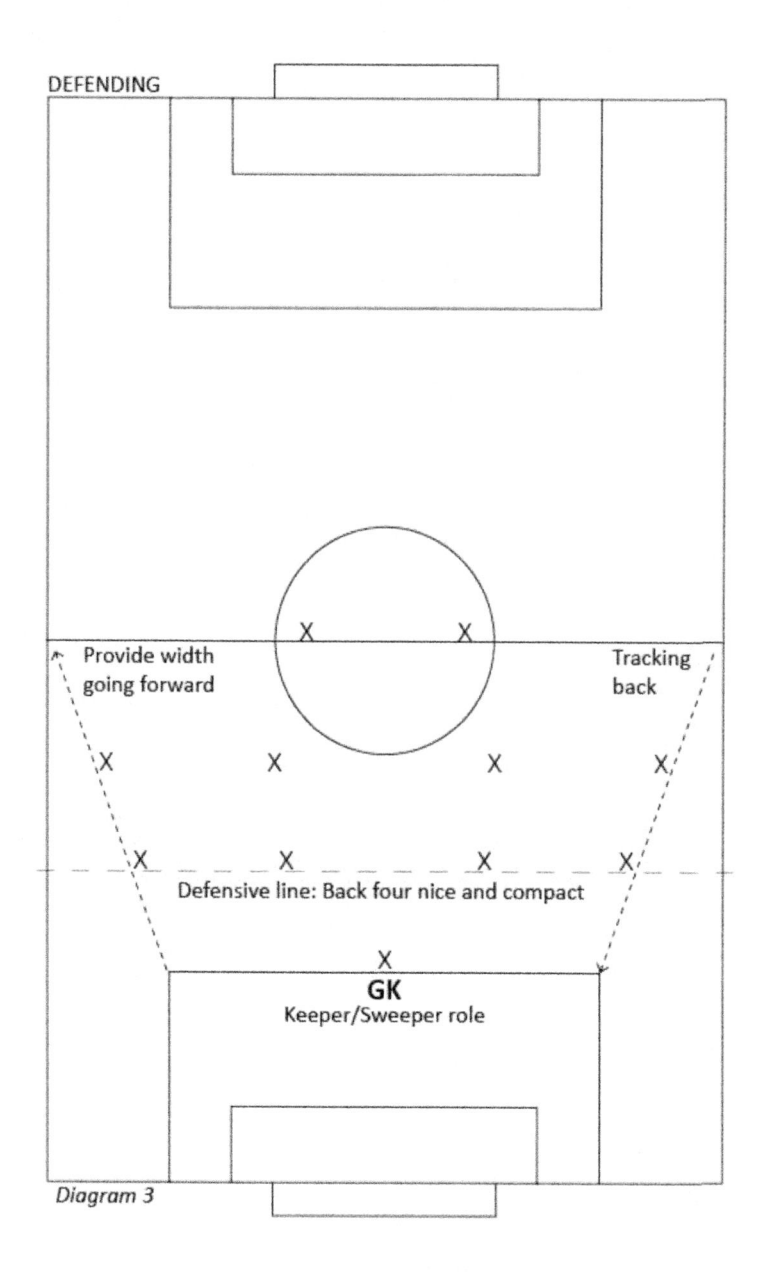

DEFENDING

Provide width going forward

Tracking back

Defensive line: Back four nice and compact

GK
Keeper/Sweeper role

Diagram 3

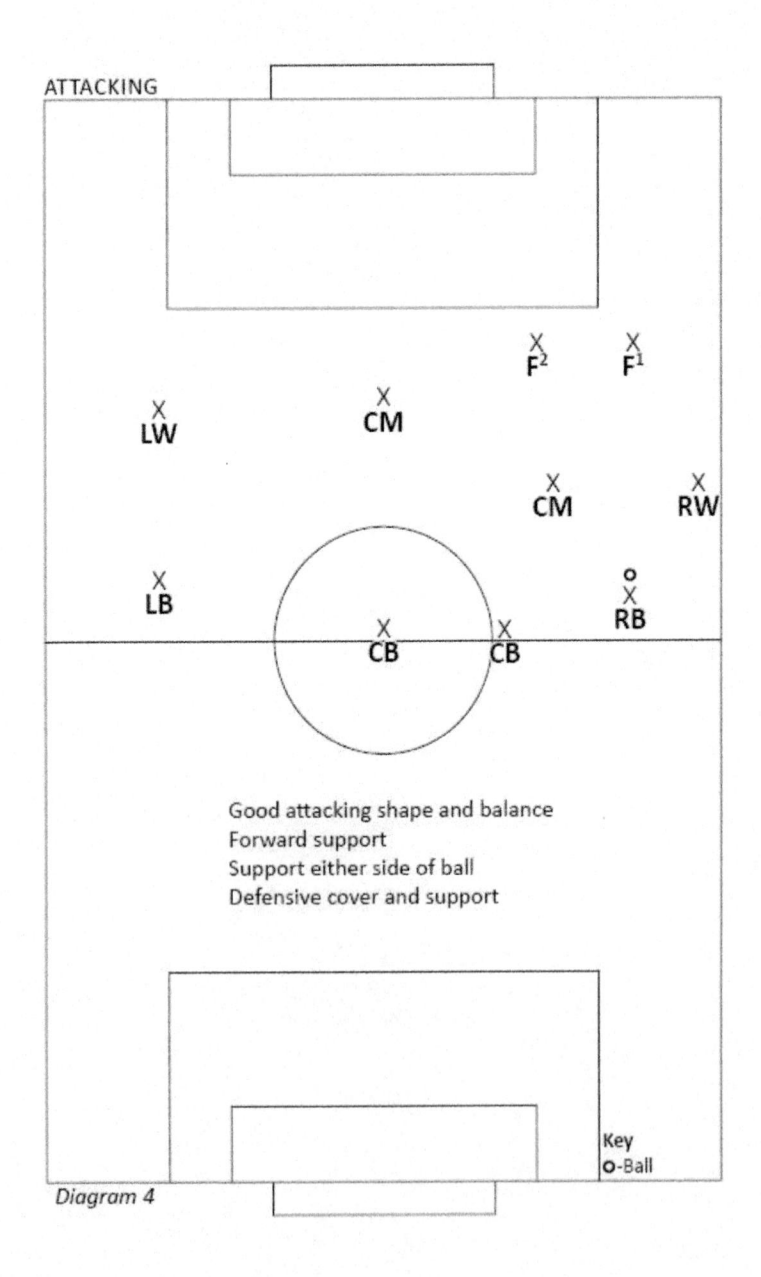

ATTACKING

F^2 F^1

LW CM

CM RW

LB RB

CB CB

Good attacking shape and balance
Forward support
Support either side of ball
Defensive cover and support

Key
o-Ball

Diagram 4

Diagram 2. Is the first thing I showed them and what I did was to divide the pitch into thirds, defending, midfield and attacking. To this, I added four channels and the system of play the coach wanted his team to play. I then proceeded to talk about good team shape and balance, pointing out that we only play with one ball and what we want to try to do is to provide good support by playing through the thirds of the pitch up and down our relevant channel.

Diagram 3. Defending Shape and Balance: Defensively, 4-4-2 gives you two banks of four with the GK playing a keeper/sweeper role. The back four are nice and compact and not too deep. The dotted lines from the halfway line back to the corner of the penalty area are a guide for the wingers tracking back. If the opposition are attacking through the middle, the two forwards will normally drop back to the halfway line. If attacking down one side, the forwards will slot over.

Diagram 4. Attacking Shape and Balance: Offensively, we are looking to stretch the opposition. Therefore, good width and depth (angles and distance of support) is the key. When the FB is on the ball (the RB or *Right-Back* in this diagram) the two forwards slot over so he now has a first and second striker he can play into. The nearest CM and winger provide support either side, creating a diamond shape and the other players provide good shape and balance.

ADE'S WAY

Soccer is a team sport. The team is only as strong as its weakest link. Don't be the weak link. Strive to be the best player you can be!

When I finished coaching at the Colchester United Youth Academy, I took up a coaching position at the Colne Community College. After my first season, it was clear that the gap between the abilities of the college players was greater than those at the pro club. With that in mind, I made a list of the areas I wanted to try to improve on during their two-year development at the college.

1. Comfortable with the ball
2. Good first touch (control and manoeuvre)
3. Control, pass and move
4. Receiving the ball (back foot)
5. Early picture
6. Decision-making
7. Forward pass/fast pass
8. Range of passing
9. Individual role (understanding)
10. Partnerships/Units
11. Team shape and balance
12. Communication (information)
13. Discipline (set pieces)

14. Support (angles and distance)
15. Attitude/Application (training and matches)
16. Competition for places
17. Performance (winning attitude)
18. Self-development
19. Trust/Respect
20. Good habits

PRINCIPLES OF SOCCER

The principles of soccer can be divided into three basic categories depending on which type of play they effect.

DEFENDING - MIDFIELD - ATTACKING

Communication is vital to successful execution in all soccer situations.

DEFENDING (Deny – Destroy – Develop)
As soon as you lose possession.

MIDFIELD (Build – Connect – Support)
The link between defending and attacking.

ATTACKING (Move – Receive – Finish)
As soon as the team gains possession.

BALL POSSESSION

ATTACKING PRINCIPLES	DEFENDING PRINCIPLES

FUNCTIONS

1. SUPPORT	1. DELAY
2. CREATION/UTILISATION OF SPACE	2. DEPTH
3. MOBILITY/WIDTH	3. BALANCE
4. ATTACKING BALANCE	4. COMPACTNESS
5. PENETRATION	5. CONCENTRATION
6. IMPROVISATION	6. CONTROL/RESTRAINT

INSTANT TRANSITION

KEEP POSSESSION	HOW TO WIN BALL BACK
WIDTH GOING FORWARD	COMPACTNESS: WHEN DEFENDING

DEFENDING

FIRST DEFENDER: A good starting position in relationship to your opponent and the ball will give you a better chance to be able to apply pressure. On your approach think, 'can I intercept, spoil or delay his forward movement?' By looping your run and closing the space down quickly, you can dictate which way you want your opponent to go. Keep your eye on the ball, stay on your feet and be prepared to jockey them until such time as you can make a solid tackle. On winning the ball you switch to attacking mode.

COVERING DEFENDER: The covering defender will take up his covering position off of the first defender. Good communication and distance are key to providing good cover. If the first defender has shown his opponent outside and he gets beat, the covering defender now becomes the first defender and applies the same principles while the first defender tries to offer support with his recovery run.

Away from the ball, the other defenders must provide good defensive shape and balance by also taking up good starting positions as well as marking and covering space.

When regaining possession of the ball and the ball is played forward, it is important to push up quickly together so as not to leave gaps.

When defending as a unit I like my back four to hold a high line and to stay nice and compact to stop penetration. Concentration and communication is the key to a well organised defence.

MIDFIELD PLAY

MIDFIELD: Referred to as the engine room, it is the link between defending and attacking. Depending on what system you adapt will dictate the roles of your midfield players. When playing three central midfielders, I am looking for a holding midfielder who will screen the back four, organise and have a good range of passing. On either side of the holding midfielder, I am looking for a creative midfielder and an attacking midfielder. The qualities I am looking for in the creative midfielder are: ability to play 360 degrees, a good first touch, comfortable in tight situations, and also has a good range of passing.

My attacking midfielder needs to be positive and forward thinking and be prepared to run at the opposition. They should have a good first touch, link-well with the front players and will get you ten to fifteen goals a season.

When playing as a unit, angles and distance of support help keep good shape and balance. In a 4–4–2, the wide players provide width and stretch the opposition's defence when going forward. Good speed endurance, a change of pace and a good supply of crosses going into the penalty area for our front players to attack, are essential. It is also very important that they have a good understanding of the defending principles looking to tuck in and to track back when the team loses possession.

ATTACKING PLAY

I have already mentioned that attacking play starts as soon as you regain possession of the ball. Movement asks questions of the opposition and good width going forward will stretch the opposition's defence. Possession doesn't win games, but it gives you a better chance, so again, good support and creating space are key factors.

I am not a lover of just playing with one up top because I think that player can get isolated. I much prefer a partnership or a unit of three. When attacking, I don't want my front players making runs into the wide channels and delivering the ball. I want my front players to look to get into the box and if we have three strikers, we are looking to attack the near post, middle of the goal and far post. When playing with two front players, I am looking for the winger on the opposite side to get in around the back looking for crosses that are over hit or knockdowns. I also say to the winger delivering the ball, 'Make sure you miss out the first defender.' To the strikers I say, 'Remember, the goal doesn't move, so make sure you work the keeper.' Whether it is a partnership or three playing up top, attacking balance and mobility is important. When playing with three up top, I like to play into our central target man, have one striker to drop off to support the layoff and the other striker looking to get in behind.

SYSTEMS OF PLAY

Obviously, it is important to have a game plan and a foundation to play from. At the pro level, where you have a scouting network, the game plan can change from game to game, depending on how the opposition sets up. The key to any system is that you have the right players in the right areas. I prefer to talk more about Shape and Balance because depending on where the ball is on the field, it can affect the system.

Good Shape and Balance comes from an understanding of your role and the application of good defending and attacking principles. Good communication and discipline is key to the execution of how your team performs. Winning your individual battles, developing good partnerships and getting the units defence, midfield and forwards working in cohesion, is what we strive for as coaches.

3 - 4 - 3

In my book *Eternal Blue Forever Green* I select my all-time Sounders team (NASL) from the players that I played with from 1974 to 1979. I have lined them up in a 3 – 4 – 3 system, which gives me good width and depth, and creates three diamonds which helps us to maintain good attacking and defending shape and balance. It also links nicely with my strategy of control–pass–move.

CHURSKY

GILLET   ENGLAND   GABRIEL

ROBERTSON   HUDSON   BUTTLE   JENKINS

CAVE   ORD   SMETHURST

Looking at my back three, they are all good solid defenders, strong in the tackle, good in the air, comfortable on the ball and all have a good range of passing, so we have no problem playing out from the back. In Gabriel, we have someone who, when the ball is played forward, can step up into the midfield and organise.

In midfield, we have a very positive unit that I know will create lots of chances. Robertson and Jenkins provide the width and I can trust them both to do the other side of the job in tucking in and tracking back when we lose possession. In Hudson and Buttle, we have two of the best to have played in the NASL. To get the best out of Huddy, I would make him my skipper and use him as my attacking midfielder, looking for him to run at the opposition and to play those combination passes off of our front men. At times, I thought Huddy could have been a bit more selfish and instead of always looking for that killer pass, get a shot off as he strikes the ball really well. Buttle would be my play maker, he is very comfortable on the ball, very seldom gives it away and he can penetrate the opposition's defence with a range of pinpoint passes. I think I would also try to work on a rotation of Buttle and Jenkins again just to ask questions of our opponents. On the right side, I would be looking for Robbo to provide the crosses, but also look to switch him from time to time, enabling him to come inside to get his shot off.

The first thing I would ask of my three front players, is to push right up on their back four as illustrated:

X O X O X O X

By playing in-between the defenders this asks questions straightaway of *who is marking who?*

Looking at my front three, I think Ordy is my best target man. He is someone you can play into and off of and is very good at holding the ball up in tight situations. I would get him to engage their central defender by getting right in underneath him. With Cave and Smethurst, I would get them to play off the shoulder of their opponent, making those darting little runs in-behind.

A pattern of play I would look to work on, would be to

get Buttle on the ball, as he plays it into Ord one of the other two drops off to receive the ball and to play it in behind for the third man to make that darting little run on to it.

So there you have it, a team that is solid at the back, playing in front of a very competent GK in Tony Chursky that can also play out from the back. The team also has a positive midfield with pace on the wings and a front three who are all proven goal scorers.

Plan B

I think it is very important to always have a Plan B. Looking at the 3–4–3 system, where I think the team might be a little vulnerable, is if the opposition play with three central midfielders and also if they play balls into the wide channels in our defensive third. In that situation, I would probably go to a 3–5–2 and bring Webster on in a holding midfield role, which would balance the overload in the centre of midfield and I would emphasise the importance of the three at the back slotting over and for the two wide players to track back.

In *Circle of Life,* I tell how during my Sounders days, we would finish every session with an 8 v 8 conditioned game (which I will explain below) and up until I retired recently, I did this with all the teams I have coached. I found it to be a really good way of creating the working, learning and fun environment that I enjoyed playing under coaches Best and Gabriel.

8 v 8

In training we finished most sessions with an 8 v 8 across half of the pitch using the full size goals. Normally the shape of both teams would be a 2 – 3 – 2 giving you two diamonds creating width and depth.

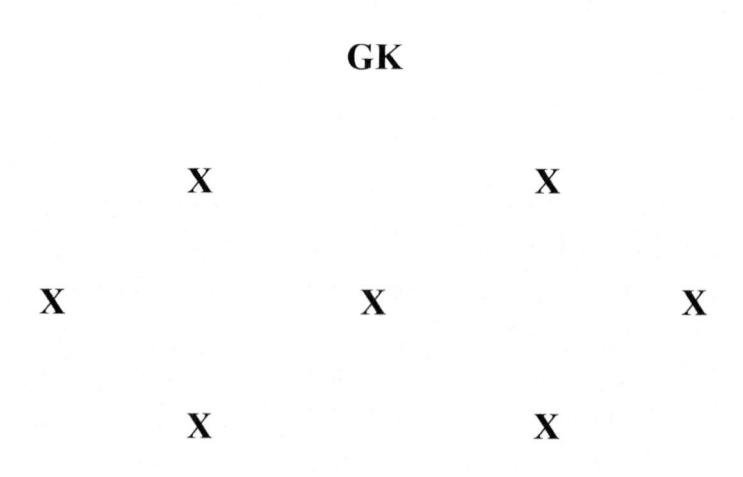

GK

      X   X

X   X   X

      X   X

The first team keeper and the reserve keeper would rotate so both would get to work with the two FBs that played together and the two CBs that were paired up. The three central midfielders would play together and link up with the two forwards.

A GUIDE TO SOCCER AND COACHING: ADE'S WAY

CHURSKY

GILLET   ENGLAND

JENKINS   WEBSTER   BUTTLE

ORD   CAVE

BUTLER   SCOTT

CROSSLEY   RUDROFF   ROBERTSON

McALISTER   MACHIN

IVANOW

What this did was to get players playing as a partnership, i.e., Gillett and England or a unit, i.e., Jenkins, Webster and Buttle. It also created lots of 1 v 1 battles. Also, as well as rotating the GKs, the coaches would put Ord and Cave up against Gillett and England. When we needed to develop our wing play, channels were added either side and our wingers would work the channels to provide crosses. The FBs would also be added into the channel so as to work on support and overlapping runs.

Conditions would also be added:

- Two touch–to move the ball quickly.
- No backward passes–to encourage passing and running the ball forward.
- Every player must be over the halfway line before your team can score a goal–to encourage your team to push up quickly together.

PATTERNS OF PLAY

SHADOW PLAY is a good way to teach how patterns of play are developed on the field so that players begin to appreciate the types of passes to make, the positions to take up, the timing of runs to coincide with the passes (and cross balls) in order to produce a successful attack. Shadow play can be used without using opposition or with just two or three players applying pressure in different areas of the pitch.

Diagram 5, build up play in the defending half: RB plays the ball into the front man who lays the ball off to the supporting CM. The CM plays the ball into the space for the RW to run onto it.

Diagram 6, build up play in the attacking half: This time the RB plays the ball into the second striker who plays the ball around the corner between the two defenders for the first striker to run onto it.

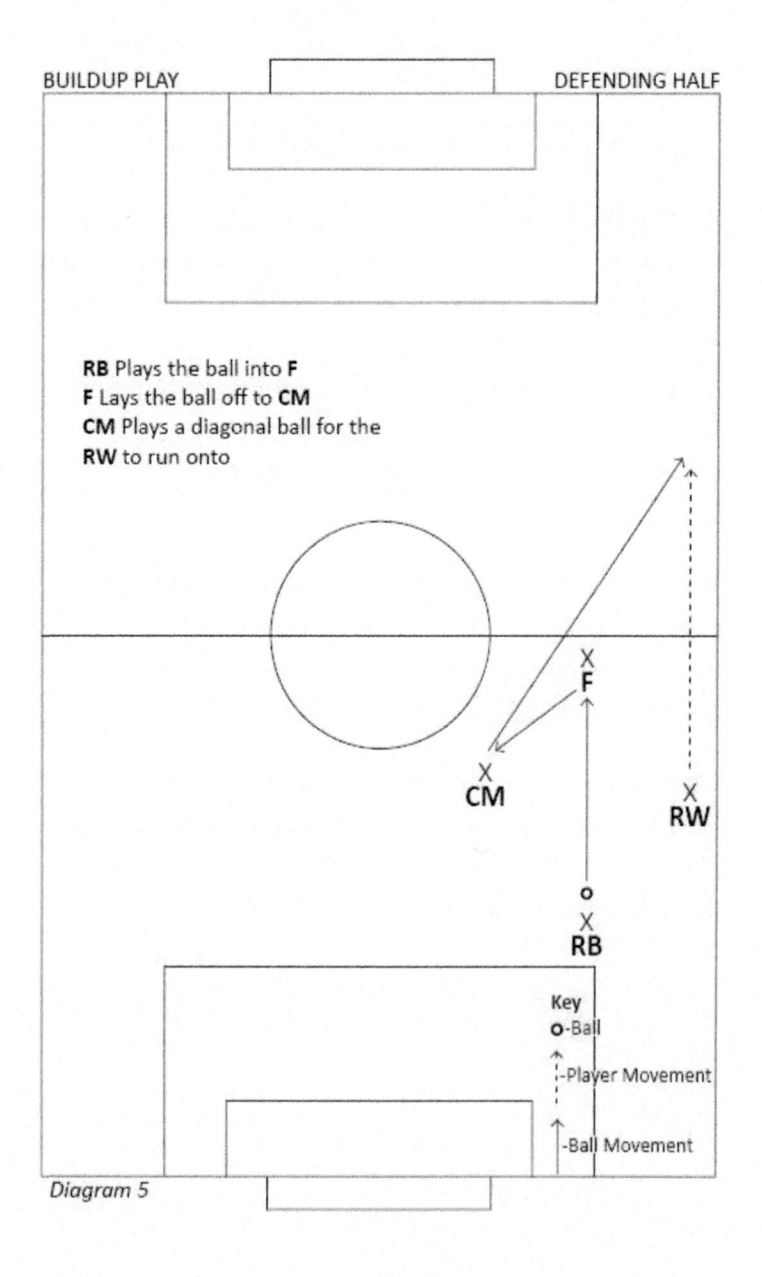

BUILDUP PLAY　　　　　　　　　　　　DEFENDING HALF

RB Plays the ball into **F**
F Lays the ball off to **CM**
CM Plays a diagonal ball for the
RW to run onto

X
F

X　　　　　　　　　X
CM　　　　　　　　RW

o
X
RB

Key
o - Ball
↑ - Player Movement
↑ - Ball Movement

Diagram 5

A GUIDE TO SOCCER AND COACHING: ADE'S WAY

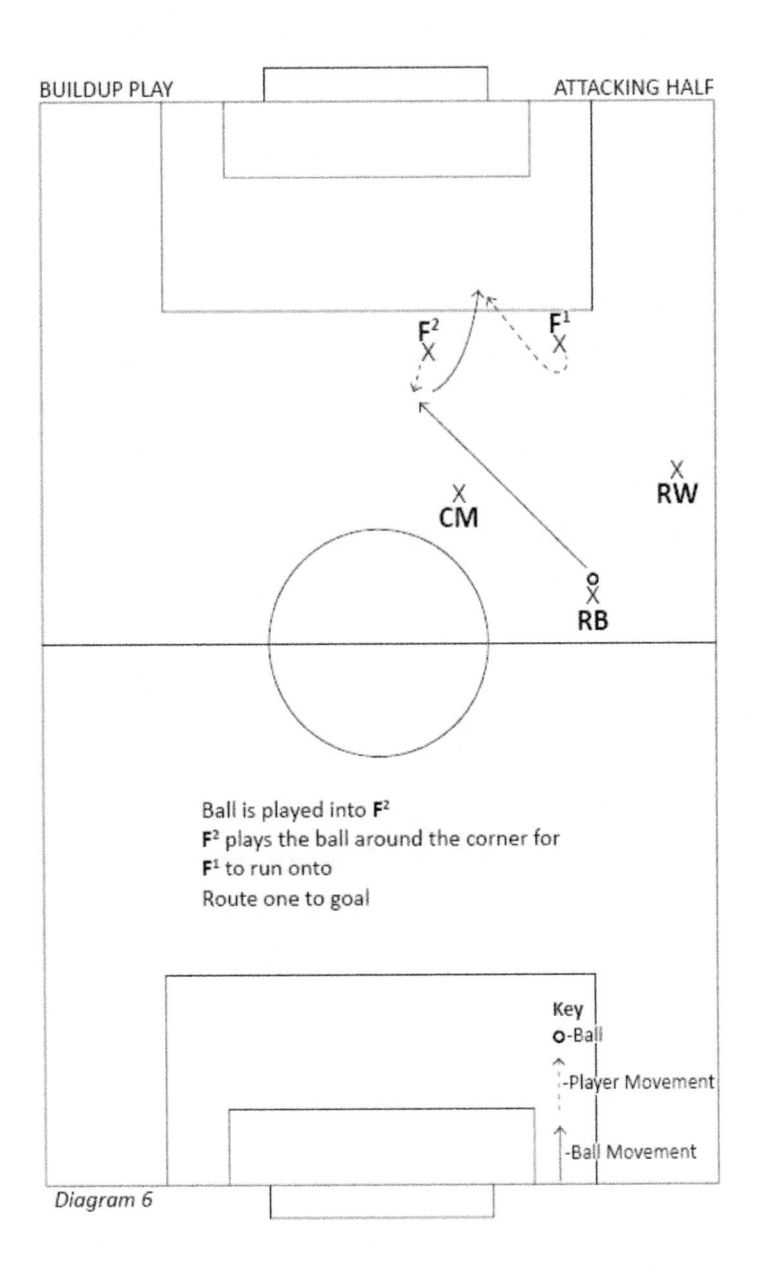

BUILDUP PLAY   **ATTACKING HALF**

F^2 F^1
X   X

X   X
RW

X
CM

o
X
RB

Ball is played into F^2
F^2 plays the ball around the corner for
F^1 to run onto
Route one to goal

Key
o - Ball
- Player Movement
- Ball Movement

Diagram 6

SET PIECES

Set pieces account for 35% of goals scored in the game. The key to good execution is to have the right players in the right areas and to have options. I always post the set pieces on the board in the dressing room before the game. That way, if someone switches off I can point the finger.

One of my pet peeves is to give the ball away too easily at throw-ins. When we get a throw-in I am looking for two things:

1. To keep possession.

2. To turn the opposition around.

Signals, communication and movement triggers which option is going to be played.

A GUIDE TO SOCCER AND COACHING: ADE'S WAY

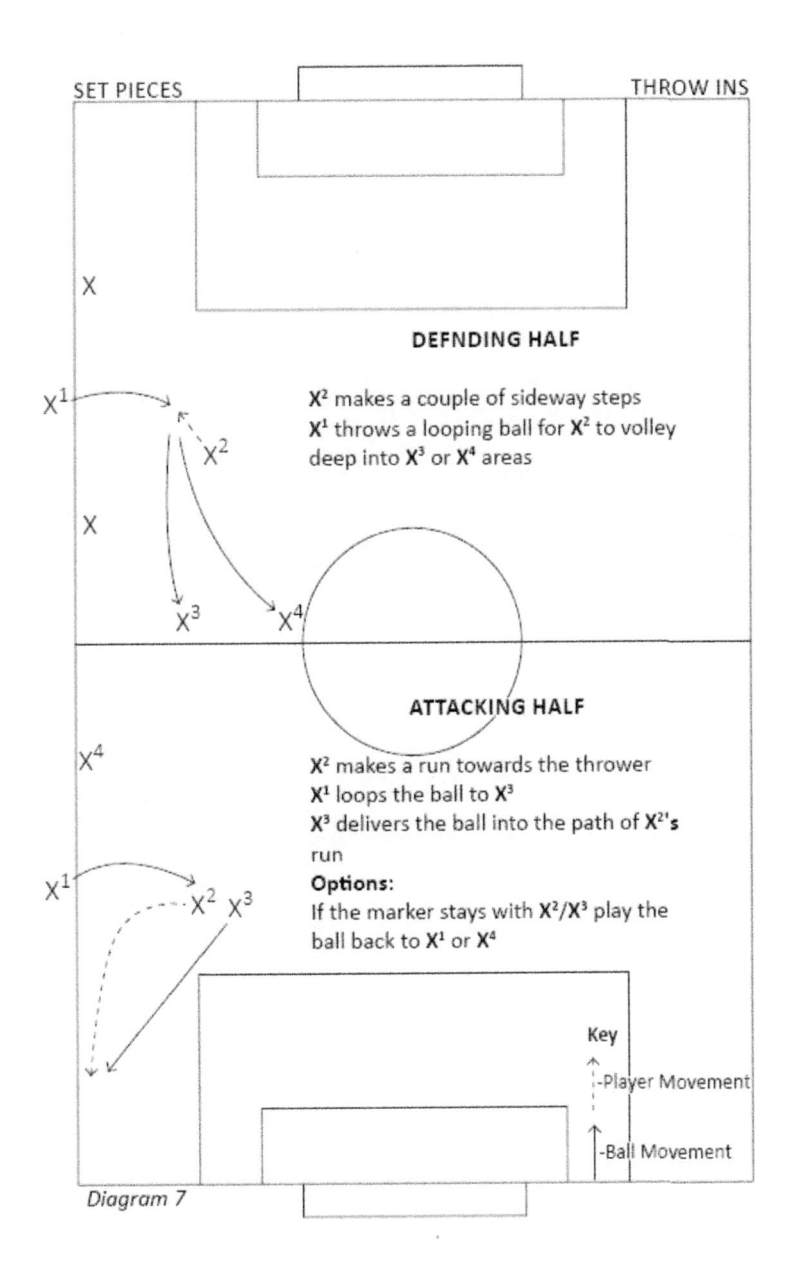

SET PIECES   **THROW INS**

DEFNDING HALF

X^2 makes a couple of sideway steps
X^1 throws a looping ball for X^2 to volley deep into X^3 or X^4 areas

ATTACKING HALF

X^2 makes a run towards the thrower
X^1 loops the ball to X^3
X^3 delivers the ball into the path of X^2's run

Options:
If the marker stays with X^2/X^3 play the ball back to X^1 or X^4

Key
- Player Movement
- Ball Movement

Diagram 7

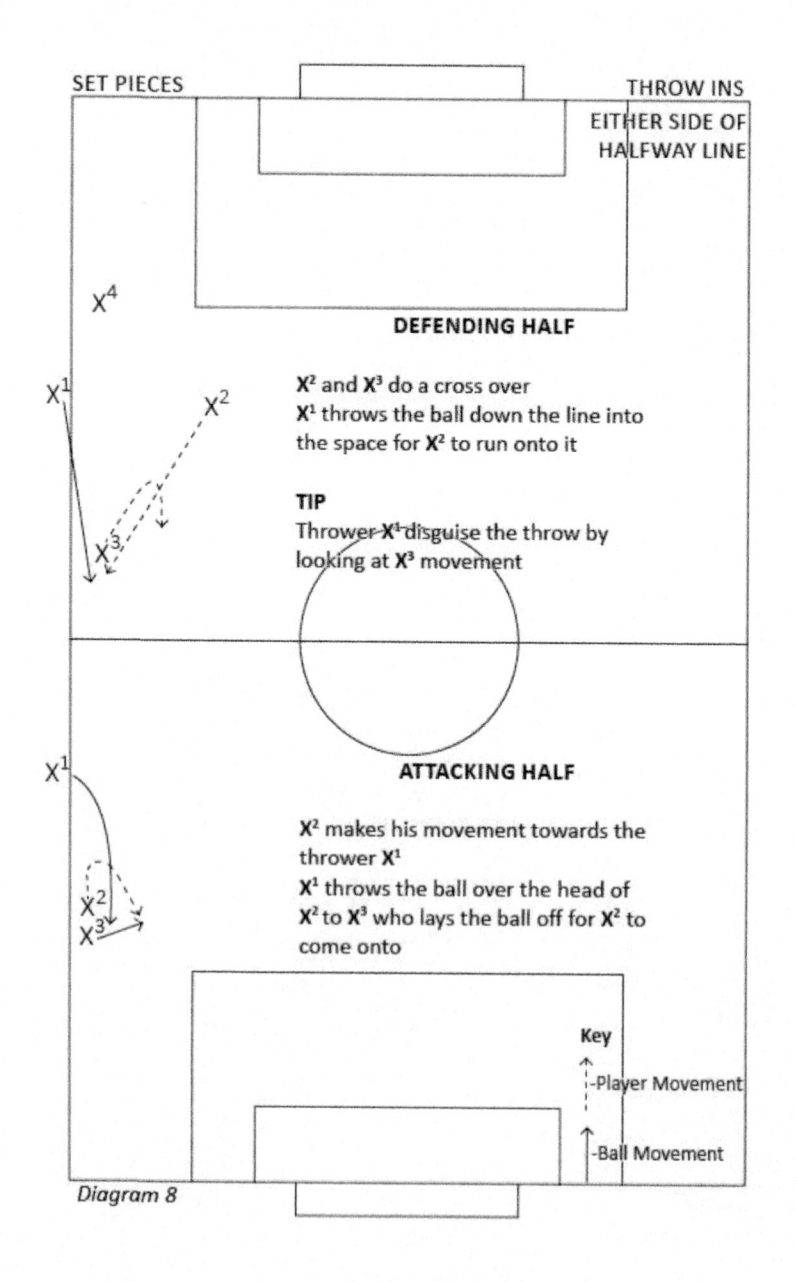

SET PIECES

THROW INS
EITHER SIDE OF HALFWAY LINE

DEFENDING HALF

X^2 and X^3 do a cross over
X^1 throws the ball down the line into the space for X^2 to run onto it

TIP
Thrower X^1 disguise the throw by looking at X^3 movement

ATTACKING HALF

X^2 makes his movement towards the thrower X^1
X^1 throws the ball over the head of X^2 to X^3 who lays the ball off for X^2 to come onto

Key
↑ -Player Movement
⇢ -Ball Movement

Diagram 8

A GUIDE TO SOCCER AND COACHING: ADE'S WAY

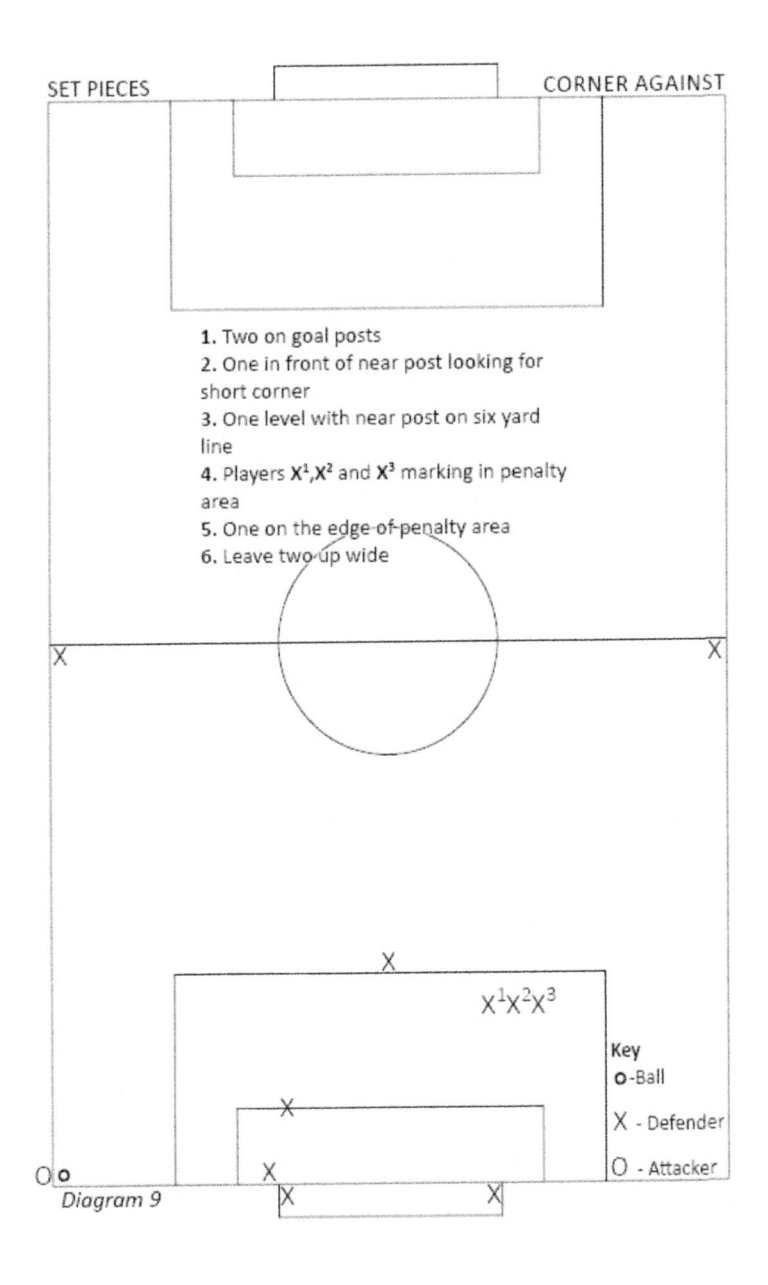

SET PIECES   **CORNER AGAINST**

1. Two on goal posts
2. One in front of near post looking for short corner
3. One level with near post on six yard line
4. Players X^1, X^2 and X^3 marking in penalty area
5. One on the edge of penalty area
6. Leave two up wide

Diagram 9

Key
o - Ball
X - Defender
O - Attacker

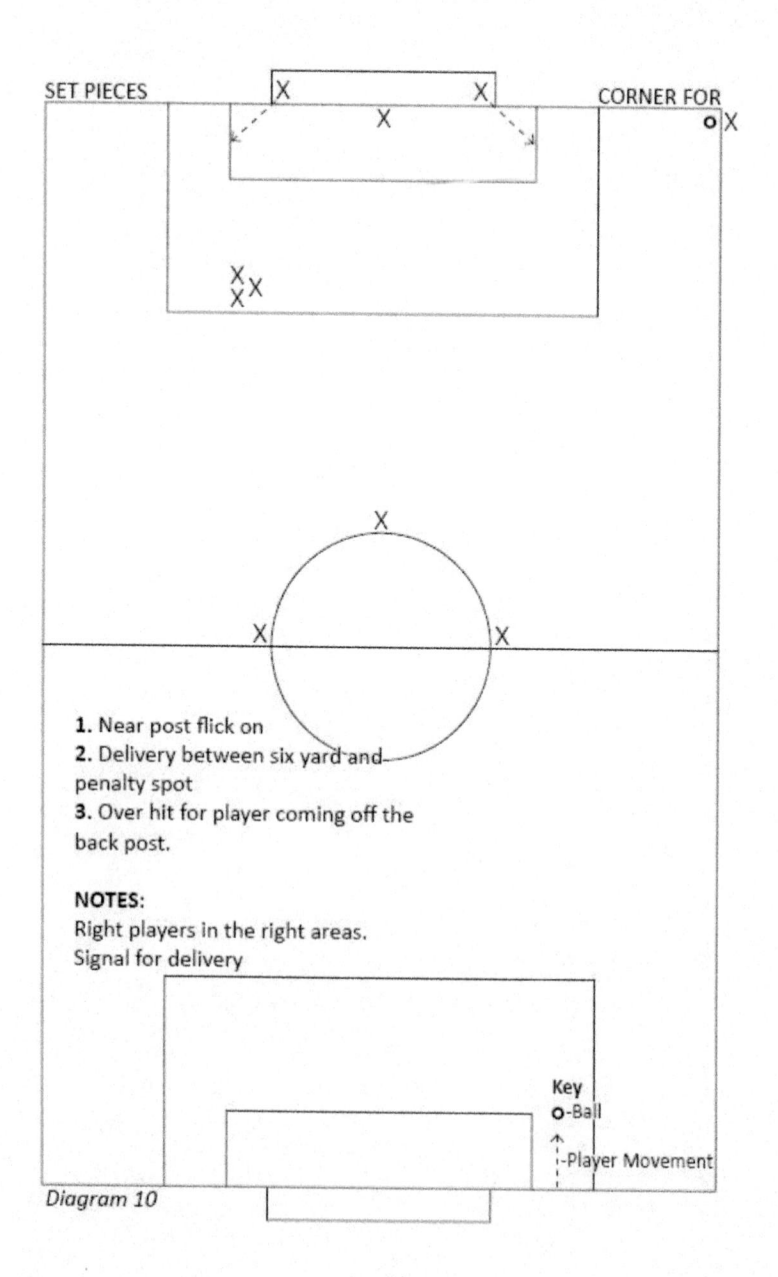

SET PIECES   CORNER FOR

1. Near post flick on
2. Delivery between six yard and penalty spot
3. Over hit for player coming off the back post.

NOTES:
Right players in the right areas.
Signal for delivery

Key
o - Ball
↑
¦ - Player Movement

Diagram 10

A GUIDE TO SOCCER AND COACHING: ADE'S WAY

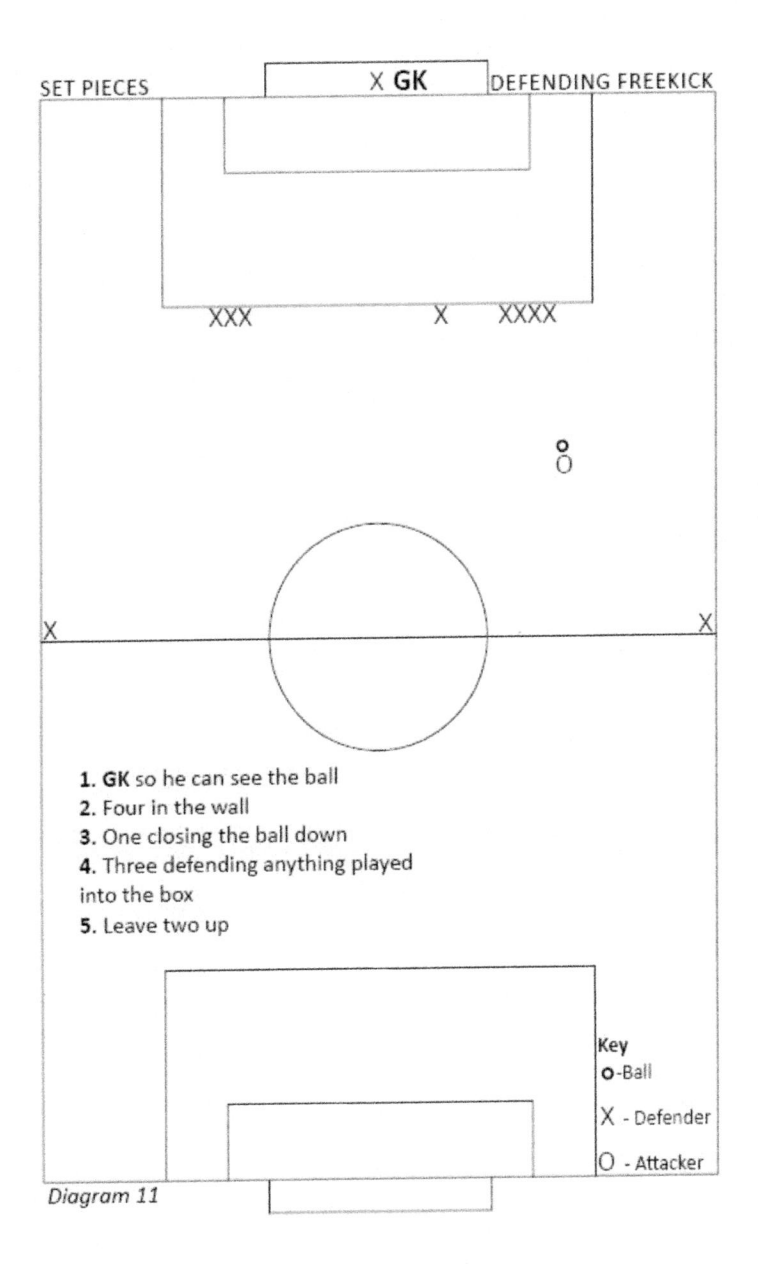

SET PIECES   X **GK**   DEFENDING FREEKICK

XXX   X   XXXX

1. **GK** so he can see the ball
2. Four in the wall
3. One closing the ball down
4. Three defending anything played into the box
5. Leave two up

Key
o - Ball
X - Defender
O - Attacker

Diagram 11

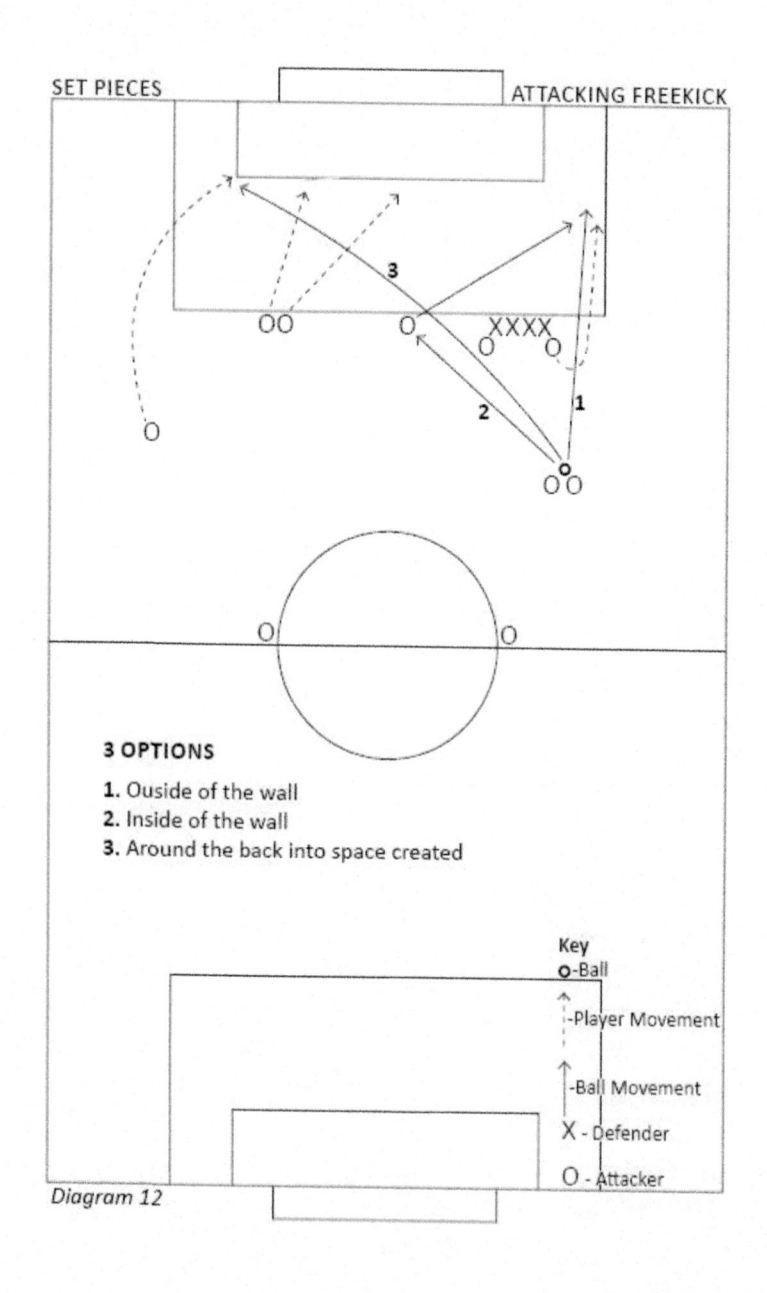

SET PIECES — ATTACKING FREEKICK

3 OPTIONS
1. Ouside of the wall
2. Inside of the wall
3. Around the back into space created

Key
O - Ball
- Player Movement
- Ball Movement
X - Defender
O - Attacker

Diagram 12

COACHING YOUTH SOCCER

As coaches, we take on a responsibility. Players need recognition, as they proceed to develop their own physical stamina, skills and tactical ability as a member of a team. The coach not only teaches, evaluates and physically prepares his players, he must be able to motivate them to fulfill their potential.

1. Teaches

2. Evaluates

3. Physically prepares

4. Motivates

What is your style?

1. Hard-nosed

2. Nice guy

3. Intense

4. Easy-going

5. Business-like

Whatever your style is, remember we are working with young players and the emphasis should be to have fun.

COACHING WITHOUT PLAYING EXPERIENCE

This is not a handicap; a playing background is not a necessity. A key to being a successful (and I don't mean winning) youth soccer coach, is to draw upon your experience. If you grew up playing sports of any kind, you possess some knowledge of good and bad coaching techniques.

DON'T

1. Become frustrated
2. Yell and intimidate
3. Be afraid to adjust your training activities if the children are not enjoying them.

DO

1. Keep players active with a ball
2. Vary the activities based upon attention span
3. Enjoy yourself
4. Be positive to all players, not just the stars.

If you are going to put some time into the development of young soccer players, you should also look at putting some time into developing yourself.

The following are some suggestions on how we can go about it:

1. Attend coaching clinics
2. Read soccer books
3. Watch higher levels of play
4. Ask and take advice of experienced coaches in your area

FINAL NOTE: As coaches we sometimes have a tendency to take the decision- making away from the players. Remember, the best teacher is the game itself. Leave the coaching until your next practice session.

ORGANISATION

A well organised session can be accomplished in 1 ½ hours.

Six to ten-year-olds   1 hour

Eleven to sixteen-year-olds 1 ½ hours

SESSION:

1. Technique (ball each)
2. Tactics (topic)
3. Conditioned game (incorporate topic)

EQUIPMENT: An adequate playing surface

YOURS	THEIRS
1. Cones/Markers	1. Ball (for teaching work)
2. Bibs	2. Shin pads
3. Stopwatch	3. Boots/Trainers
4. Balls/Pump	4. Appropriate clothing

Stretching should be done as a warm-up before training and a warm down after training.

I believe at the youth level, the emphasis should be put on technical ability.

COMPONENTS OF SOCCER

1. **Technique**
2. **Tactics**
3. **Physical Fitness**
4. **Physiology (Mental Alertness)**

TECHNIQUE

Coaching basic skills is based on a progressive pattern beginning with the fundamentals and leading to the more complex method of dealing with the ball.

EXAMPLE: Teaching passing technique

PROGRESSION: Fundamental - in twos

Match related - 5 v 2

Match condition - 5 v 5 two touch

BASIC SKILLS

1. Ball juggling (to develop touch)

2. Passing

3. Shooting

4. Heading

5. Dribbling

6. Tackling

7. Control

BALL JUGGLING: When I first got into coaching I was asked to warm-up a group of players that each had a ball. So I got them juggling the ball using the various body parts—feet, thighs and head. After about five minutes, the tutor came over and said to me "Do you see players in the game standing there juggling the ball?" I replied, *"No."* Then he said, *"So make it more game specific and get the players moving with the ball."* I thought straightaway that made sense, however I do think juggling the ball is a good exercise to help improve your touch and balance and gets you using both sides of your body.

PASSING: All players, especially from an early age, should be encouraged to use both feet. Whether it is a dead ball situation or a moving ball, the weight of the pass is the most important ingredient because even though you might be a little off with your pass, if the weight is right, the receiver can still get there. Basically, there are three types of passes 1. Push pass 2. Driven pass. 3. Chip or Lofted pass.

The Push pass is played with the inside of the foot over a short distance. On contact with the ball drop your bottom, this will help take the bobble out of the pass and keep it low. The Driven pass is played with pace using the lace area of your boot and the Chip or Lofted pass is when you want to get the ball up and over an obstruction using the big toe area of your foot. When making the pass the decision is whether to play the ball into feet or space.

SHOOTING: While coaching the U16 Youth Academy team at Colchester United, I attended a coaching seminar in Newcastle–Upon–Tyne, in the north of England. One of the topics on the course was shooting and one of the senior coaches put on a shooting session. He started by selecting ten players who were all ex pros. He asked them to hit a half volley from about twenty yards out, trying to beat the GK by aiming for the corners of the goal. One or two found the corners, but most hit the ball wide of the goal. He then asked them to try to hit the GK on the knees with the ball. Again, one or two hit the target but this time most of the shots went into the corner of the goal.

With young players, I tell them to make sure they hit the target and to follow up on all shots. Players have to remember the goal doesn't move, so when taking a touch, first try to set the ball to give yourself a good angle to get a quick shot off. If going near post with your shot, hit it hard and high at the GK. When in a wide position, hit it hard and low across the GK.

HEADING: With defensive heading, you are looking for height and distance. Therefore, keep the head steady and head the ball slightly below centre using the forehead. A lot of players struggle because they expect the ball to drop perfectly on their head. Read the flight of the ball, work your feet and jump towards the ball.

When I was an apprentice at Colchester, the trainer, Denis Mochan, would have a bag of balls in the centre circle. We would start inside the penalty area and he would hit balls in the air for us to come onto and head clear. We did this a couple of times a week, heading between ten and twenty balls per session.

ATTACKING HEADING: This time you are looking to guide the ball down to a teammate, or past the GK when in an attacking position. Therefore, we want to head the ball slightly above centre. For this, Denis would serve the ball in from the goal post , changing posts after ten headers. We would start our run from the edge of the penalty area and meet the ball between the penalty spot and six-yard box. He would then progress it by getting the wingers to cross the balls in from wide positions. We were taught that when the winger put his head down to cross the ball, make your first movement away from the ball and then come back onto it. We would also work on glancing headers but most times as the GK came from his starting position, we would be looking to head the ball back in the direction he had come from.

DRIBBLING: When I think about dribbling, the first name that comes to mind is George Best. George had tremendous balance and was very brave which can be seen on a lot of the footage of him playing for Manchester Utd. He had great close control, the ability to feint and dummy his opponent, a change of pace and the ability to change direction. He was very positive in his play and it can be measured in the number of goals he scored and the assists he had. There are a lot of players that are good at running and dribbling with the ball but have no end product. In contrast, not only did George score and setup goals, he won free kicks, corner kicks and at the end of a dazzling run, he usually forced the keeper into making an incredible save.

Having played against George on a few occasions, I always felt it was best to try to stop him from turning because once he got turned, he would turn you inside out. When playing against top players like George, you always try to force them onto their weak side. But George had two great feet.

Simple attacking principles: **Create.** **Maintain. Exploit.**

TACKLING: At times I think defenders feel that they have to try to win every ball when the first thing they should do, is to make sure they are goal side and ball side of the player they are marking. The best time to get your tackle in is as your opponent is half turned with the ball.

BLOCK TACKLE: In a 50/50 challenge for the ball, lower your centre of gravity, stay on your feet and when making your challenge, lean into your tackle to get your full weight behind it.

SLIDE TACKLE: Defenders are encouraged not to go to ground but to stay on their feet. Usually a slide tackle is more of a desperation tackle where you are stretching for the ball. The best place to make a sliding tackle is close to the touch line where you are less likely to get caught out.

CONTROL: There are two ways of bringing the ball under control 1. Cushion Control and 2. Wedge Control.

CUSHION CONTROL: Try to get your body in line with the ball. Select the surface you intend to use foot, thigh, chest or head. On contact relax the body part, i.e. If using your head bend through your legs. Ideally you want to control the ball into the space slightly in front of you.

WEDGE CONTROL: Again get behind the line of the ball and by placing your foot or chest over the ball you stop it from bouncing backup at you.

When controlling the ball, your first touch is important. Think 'control and manoeuvre' which will give you a little bit more space and time. If your first touch is forward, be positive and look to run or pass the ball forward.

HOW TO SETUP

I think the key to a productive session is to utilise the time you have available with the players. Below, is the structure I learned at my F.A. Coaching License (UEFA 'B' Award) I attended when I first returned from the States.

1. Introduce topic
2. Organise
3. Demonstrate
4. Sufficient practice
5. Correct problems
6. Summarise
7. Next stage

TACTICS

WHAT ARE TACTICS?

1. Tactics come into play when there is opposition.
2. Competing for ball possession.
3. Recognition of options and making decisions.

PROGRESSION:

Individual Tactics	1 v 1
Group Tactics	2 v 1 2 v 2 2 v 3
	3 v 1 3 v 3 4 v 2 4 v 3 4 v 4
	5 v 4 5 v 5
Team Tactics	6 v 4 through 11 v 11

INDIVIDUAL TACTICS: To improve and develop a players' ability to handle the 1 v 1 situation that is common in soccer.

GROUP TACTICS: Learning what to do as a group around the ball is the objective of group tactics.

TEAM TACTICS: In teaching team tactics, the coach must concentrate on both the individual performance and combination play. He must mold a unit of up to eleven players that will have the capacity of both attacking and defending.

The use of restriction is a valuable method of teaching team tactical play.

COACHING GRID: The grid is usually marked off in either a square or a rectangular shape and is used to work on a tactical problem.

COMPETING FOR BALL POSSESSION

Individual	Restricted Area	Grid	Tactics when there is opposition
Group	To one goal	Direction	Match related
Team	To two goals	Counter Attack	Match condition

PHYSICAL FITNESS

Physical fitness training involves exposing the body to higher levels of work than it is accustomed to.

The Integral components of physical conditioning are:

1. Endurance

2. Strength

3. Flexibility

4. Speed

5. Coordination

6. Agility

ENDURANCE: Sustaining an effort without undue fatigue over a period of time.

STRENGTH: Maximal force or power of which involved muscles are capable.

FLEXIBILITY: The range of motion possible at a joint.

SPEED: The ability to move from one point to another

in the least possible time.

COORDINATION: To perform a skill as efficiently as possible without wasting body movement.

AGILITY: The ability to move with quickness and ease. (Change direction with and without ball).

METHODS OF TRAINING

INTERVAL TRAINING: Short work bouts interspersed with rest periods.

CIRCUIT TRAINING: Continuous work involving different muscle groups.

FARTLEK: Continuous running while changing speeds.

PRESSURE TRAINING: Another form of interval training. Technique under pressure of time and fatigue.

ECONOMICAL TRAINING: Training sessions that combine at least two of the four basic components of soccer.

FUNCTIONAL TRAINING: Is specialized in the particular skills necessary for playing a specific position. Training under game conditions that stresses a player's technical or tactical weakness.

The three running exercises in Diagrams 13 and 14 are variations of many different running exercises I did as a player and use as a coach.

Doing the Star Run with the ball gets the players working at getting the ball out from under their feet as well as taking their mind off of the run and without the ball it helps their endurance.

Speed Endurance is important when you make a forward run. It breaks down and you have to get back quickly.

Game Specific run incorporates the different types of runs you make in a game, forward, backwards and sideways.

The above two also highlight a change of pace and direction used when trying to lose your opponent.

ADRIAN WEBSTER

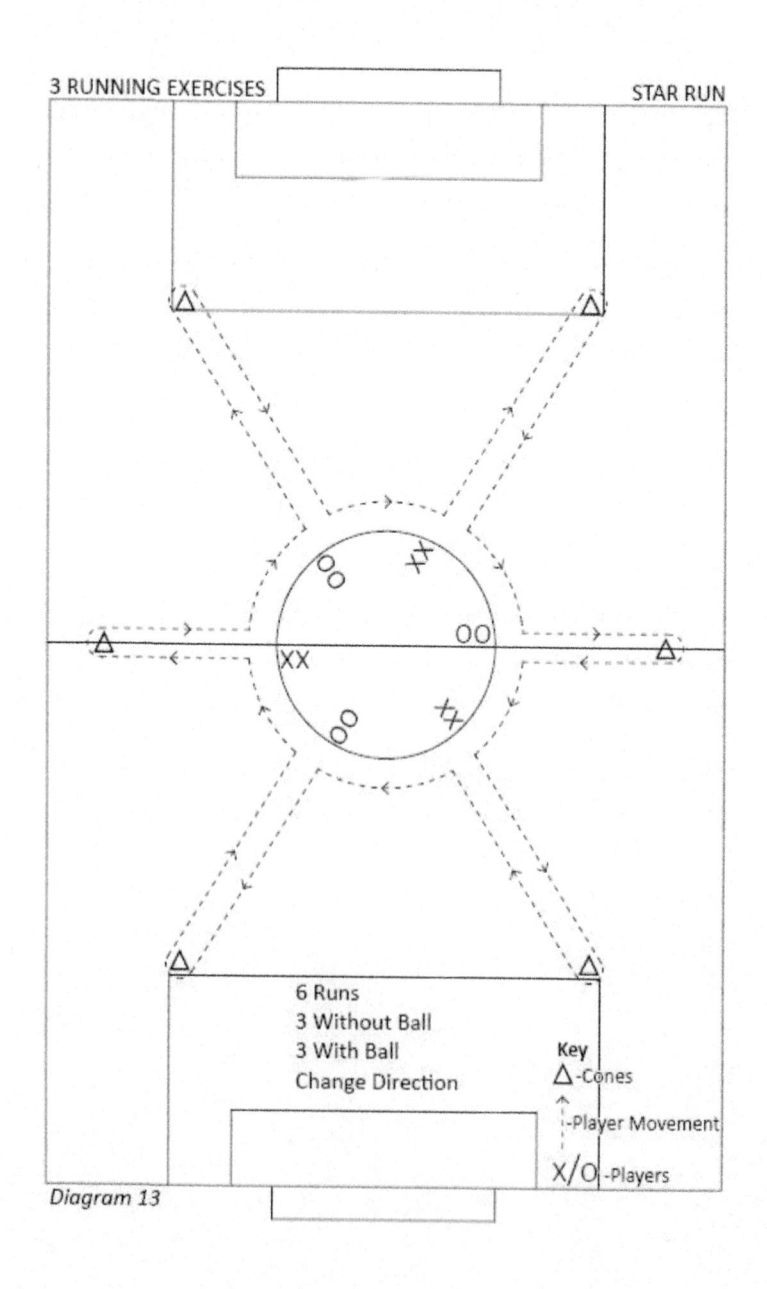

3 RUNNING EXERCISES
STAR RUN

6 Runs
3 Without Ball
3 With Ball
Change Direction

Key
△ - Cones
- Player Movement
X/O - Players

Diagram 13

A GUIDE TO SOCCER AND COACHING: ADE'S WAY

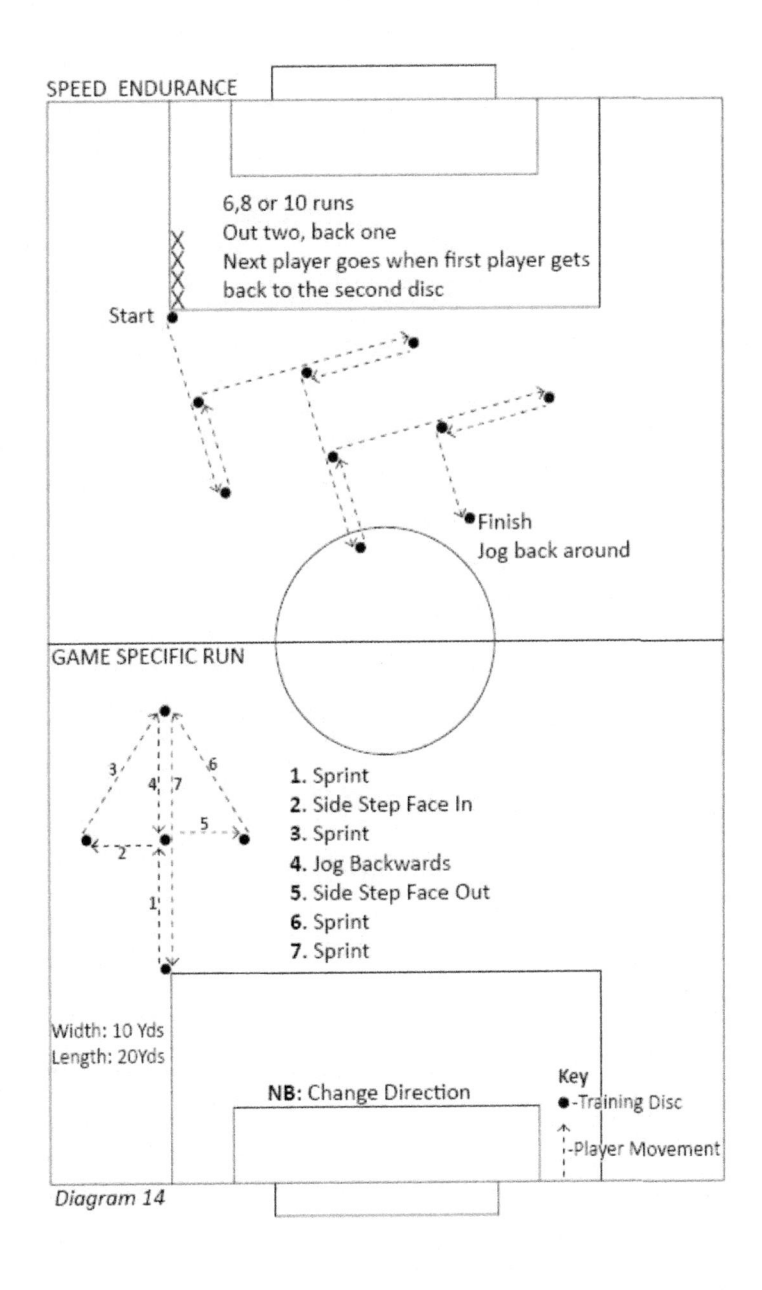

SPEED ENDURANCE

6, 8 or 10 runs
Out two, back one
Next player goes when first player gets back to the second disc

Start

Finish
Jog back around

GAME SPECIFIC RUN

1. Sprint
2. Side Step Face In
3. Sprint
4. Jog Backwards
5. Side Step Face Out
6. Sprint
7. Sprint

Width: 10 Yds
Length: 20 Yds

NB: Change Direction

Key
● - Training Disc
↑
¦ - Player Movement

Diagram 14

PSYCHOLOGY–MENTAL ALERTNESS

As coaches, we want to try to get the best out of our players.

We must remember that when working with youth players, they are all striving to develop their own identity, so how we deal with one individual may not be the right approach for another. This is an interesting part of the game and can be very frustrating.

As players get tired, they begin to make mistakes. This is when the psychological dimension is tested; who has that mental toughness to battle on even when making mistakes and to continue to run, work and talk.

Coach Best in his pre–game talk, would always say it was about winning your individual battles and that if he had seven players winning their battles, we always had a chance of winning the game, knowing on the day one or two might have an off day.

Today, there are lots of debates about the pressure put on young players to win. My personal feeling is that up to the age of eleven, the emphasis should be on technical development. I do believe that a player's development is ongoing, and I do not see anything wrong in trying to develop a winning mentality. Even today, when I am playing games with my grandchildren, I play to try to win. As you move up the ladder as a player, coach or manager, winning games is how you are judged, and I think you should use losing a game as an incentive to do better and work harder.

PRE-SEASON

In 1981, I went to Arizona to play for the Phoenix Inferno in the MISL (Major Indoor Soccer League). It was a new franchise and initially, because we did not have a training facility, we did our pre-season outdoors on a running track. Because of the heat, we did the running in the morning, followed by an upper body session at a local gym. The ball work we did in the afternoons over at a local park. Five weeks into our training program, the Inferno installed a temporary playing surface with surrounding boards in the car park at the stadium where we would play our regular season games.

Norm Sutherland was the general manager and he brought in a fitness coach to do the conditioning. I helped with the ball work as I had played for the Pittsburgh Spirit the previous season and the indoor game was new to some of the players Norm had recruited.

I really enjoyed the conditioning program and over the years, I have used this format with the players I have worked with.

WEEK 1. Monday – Friday. Warm up. 12 minute run on grass track (looking each day to improve your distance). Gym – upper body and core work.

Afternoon session ball work and conditioned games.

WEEK 2. Monday – Friday. Warm up 3 running groups on grass 220 yards.
Vary the number of runs each day (6 on day one, 8 on day two, 10 on day three, 8 on day four, 6 on day five). By increasing the number of runs and then decreasing them come Friday you are flying. Gym – upper body and core work. Afternoon session ball work and conditioned games.

WEEK 3. Monday – Friday. Warm up 3 running groups on grass 100 yard sprints 6,8,10,8,6. Gym – upper body and core work. Afternoon session ball work and conditioned games.

WEEK 4. Monday – Friday. Warm up 3 running groups on grass 30 yard sprints 6,8,10,8,6. Gym – upper body and core work. Afternoon session ball work and conditioned games.

WEEKS 5 and 6 were done at the temporary training facility and the work we did was all game specific to the indoor game. We also played 4 pre-season games.

As you can see the format follows a progressive pattern whereby we were looking to get sharper as the season got closer. In the training games we worked on playing two minute shifts playing at a high tempo and getting use to the part the boards played tactically.

SUMMARY

"The Beautiful Game" as Pele once called it, is still the biggest game played all over the world. As well as the men's game, women's soccer has also come on leaps and bounds over the last couple of decades.

When I was growing up, the fields on the estate where I lived were packed with games being played, from 2 v 2 to 15 v 15 with no referees or coaches. My first taste of being coached was by our PE teacher who happened to be an ex-pro. Fortunately, soccer was big in the schools and the progression was from school to district and county football. If you were good enough and you had a pro club in the town or city where you lived, you might be one of the lucky ones to be offered an apprenticeship.

Today, the system is very different, and a lot of school football has been replaced by club football which is played on Sundays. Most pro clubs now have academies, development programs and community projects. Therefore, there is a greater need for more coaches and for coaches to move up the ladder.

The question that is often asked is, with all the infrastructure now in place, are we (in England) producing quality players and teams. I think that is a lengthy debate, but what I would say is that we now live in a different society. Things have changed and although I enjoy watching many of the foreign players playing over here, I can't help but feel it has restricted our young players from progressing. Also, for some reason, we are not producing the quality coaches and managers.

I started the book by saying I thought there were already lots of coaching resources out there and as I looked through what I had written, I started to question what I was reading and saying. When I read my first draft of the book, I realised I had already made that point, and considered taking it out. However, when I thought about it a bit more, I decided to leave it in to emphasise the point because for me, coaching or training is about repetition doing it day in and day out until it becomes second nature. Training is about developing good habits and the game is the platform to express your soccer skills individually and collectively.

MY TEN SOCCER COMMANDMENTS

1. **Touch -** Comfortable with the ball.

2. **Control -** Receiving the ball using feet, thighs, chest and head.

   Cushion / Wedge. Get the ball out from under your feet.

3. **Range of passing -** Use both feet. *Push pass, Driven pass* and *Lofted pass.*
   Pass consideration:
   i. To feet
   ii. Into space
   iii. Accuracy
   iv. Weight / Pace

4. **Running with the ball**
   i. Out from under your feet
   ii. Positive
   iii. Change of pace
   iv. Change of direction

5. **Winning the ball -**
    i. Tackling
    ii. Interception
    iii. Steal

6. **Heading - Defensive:** Height and Distance.

    Offensive: Head downwards.

7. **Win individual battles -** Compete.

8. **Partnerships -** Angle and Distance of Support Covering position and Communication.

9. **Unit -** Communication, Width and Depth.

10. **Team Shape and Balance -** Understanding of individual roles.

DEFENDING AND ATTACKING PRINCIPLES

DEFENDING

1. Body Shape

2. Eye on the Ball

3. Stay on your feet

4. Jockey

ATTACKING

1. Movement with and without ball

2. Keep the ball moving

3. Pace/Tempo

4. End product

SPECIAL THANKS

I would like to thank Dr Alex Gillett (a cousin of Sounders legend Dave Gillett), a Lecturer at University of York's Management School, who has previously published research on soccer and it's history. Alex read my work and provided advice on some of the content.

Also, Oliver Hatton 'an Art Student 'Graduate of Colchester Institute, who helped me with the diagrams in the book and with my improving IT skills.

ABOUT THE AUTHOR

ADRIAN WEBSTER

Adrian Webster played for the Seattle Sounders NASL '74 - '79. As a young lad growing up in England, his favourite players were Pele and George Best.

In 1977, Head Coach Jimmy Gabriel made him team captain and that season he lead his team to the Soccer Bowl Final in Portland. On the way to the final, he was voted Man of the Match for his man-marking performance on George Best and in the final he came up against his other idol, Pele.

During his six seasons with the Sounders, he played with and against some of the greats of that era.

Look for Adrian Webster's Other Books

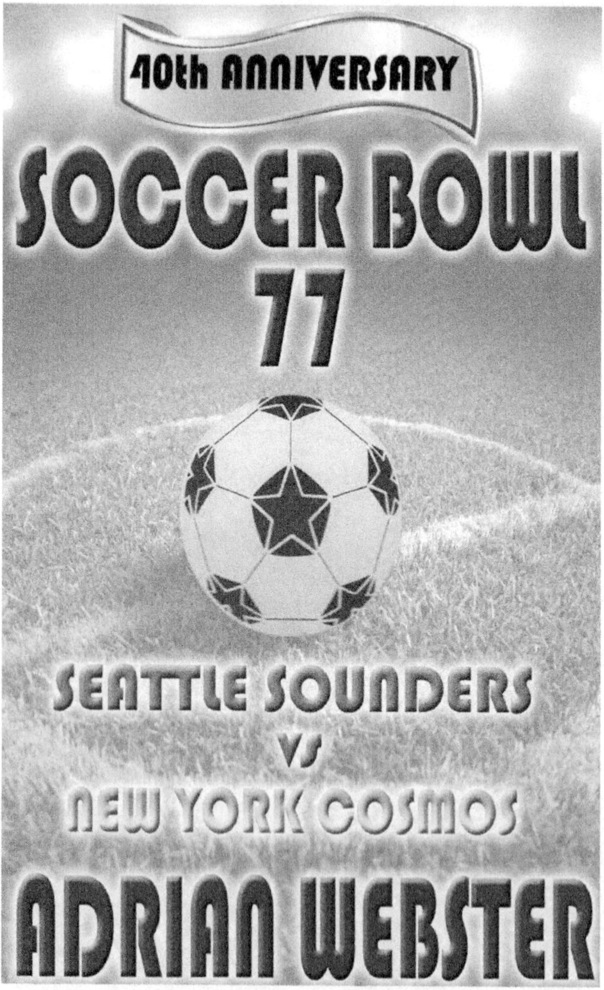
40th ANNIVERSARY
SOCCER BOWL
77
SEATTLE SOUNDERS
VS
NEW YORK COSMOS
ADRIAN WEBSTER

A GUIDE TO SOCCER AND COACHING: ADE'S WAY

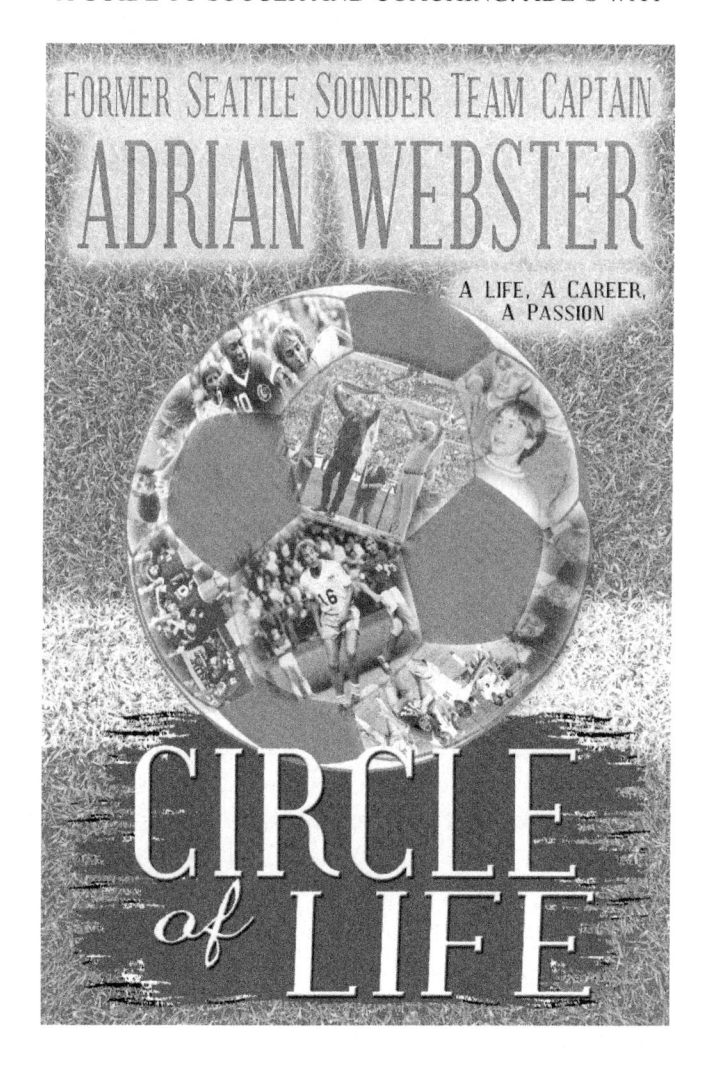

Available in paperback and all the eBook platforms.

Books to Go Now

You can find more stories such as this at
www.bookstogonow.com

If you enjoy this Books to Go Now story please leave a review for the author on a review site which you purchased the eBook. Thanks!

We pride ourselves with representing great stories at low prices. We want to take you into the digital age offering a market that will allow you to grow along with us in our journey through the new frontier of digital publishing. Some of our favorite award-winning authors have now joined us. We welcome readers and writers into our community.

We want to make sure that as a reader you are supplied with never-ending great stories. As a company, Books to Go Now, wants its readers and writers supplied with positive experience and encouragement so they will return again and again.

We want to hear from you. Our readers and writers are the cornerstone of our company. If there is something you would like to say or a genre that you would like to see, please email us at inquiry@bookstogonow.com